Tie Dip Dye

Pepa Martin and Karen Davis

D&C
David and Charles

www.stitchcraftcreate.co.uk

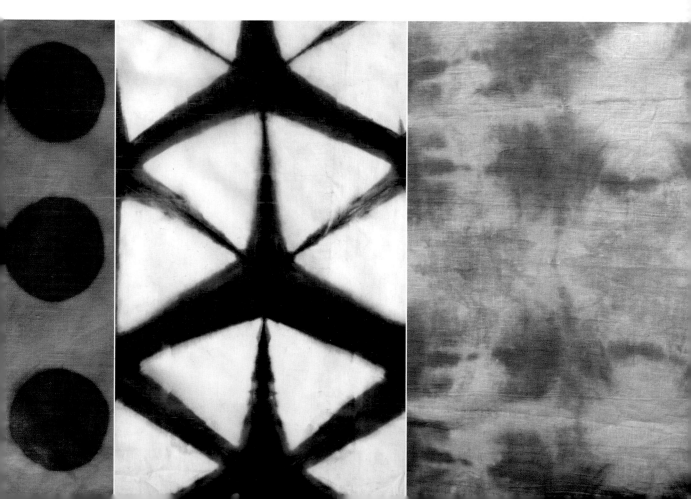

A DAVID & CHARLES BOOK

David & Charles is an imprint of
F&W Media International, Ltd
Brunel House, Forde Close, Newton Abbot,
TQ12 4PU, UK

F&W Media International, Ltd is a
subsidiary of F+W Media, Inc
10151 Carver Road, Suite #200, Blue Ash,
OH 45242, USA

First published in the UK and USA in 2015

ISBN-13: 978-1-4463-0487-7
ISBN-10: 1-4463-0487-6

F+W Media publishes high quality books on a wide
range of subjects. For more great book ideas visit:
www.stitchcraftcreate.co.uk

QUAR.FTDP

Conceived, designed and produced by
Quarto Publishing plc, The Old Brewery, 6 Blundell
Street, London N7 9BH

Project editor: Chelsea Edwards • Art editor: Jackie
Palmer • Designer: Simon Brewster • Photographer:
Luisa Brimble • Stylist: John Mangila • Illustrator:
John Woodcock • Copy editor: Ruth Patrick • Picture
researcher: Sarah Bell • Proofreader: Corinne
Masciocchi • Indexer: Helen Snaith • Art director:
Caroline Guest • Creative director: Moira Clinch •
Publisher: Paul Carslake

Color separation in Hong Kong by:
Cyprus Colours (HK) Ltd
Printed in China by:
1010 Printing International Ltd

10 9 8 7 6 5 4 3 2 1

Contents

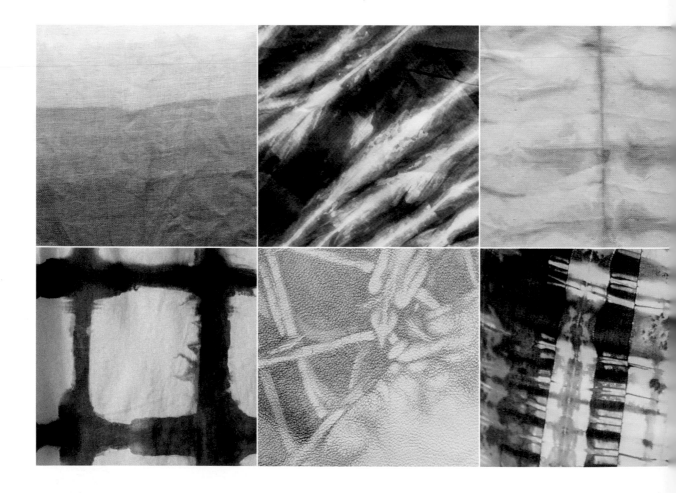

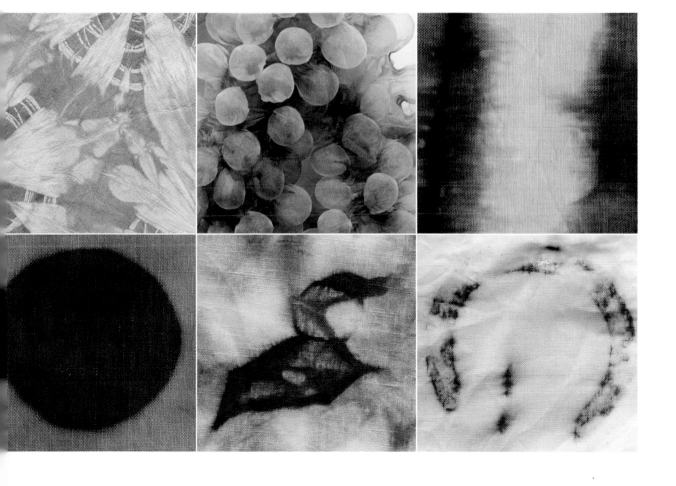

About this book

This book has twelve techniques, each with three variations to show that there are no hard-and-fast rules in the world of dyeing. Mix and match the different techniques, dyes and folding formations to create uniquely beautiful pieces. In addition, every technique is accompanied by a project for you to try your hand at, from an arashi tote bag to a dip-dyed dress.

At the beginning of the book, a chapter on the essential tools and materials, as well as design placement and colour considerations, will help you to get the most from the dyeing process.

GETTING STARTED
This chapter seeks to help you gain the best results from the dyeing process by ensuring you're equipped with the correct tools and materials. Also detailed are a number of the key dye recipes used throughout the book.

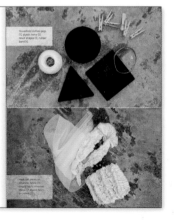

PLEATING DIAGRAMS
Clear diagrams demonstrate the most common folding techniques referred to in the book.

INTRODUCTION AND TOOLS
A brief contextualization of the technique is included here, along with a list of all the tools and equipment you'll need.

STEP-BY-STEP SEQUENCES
Concise steps are given to help you replicate each technique at home. Colour photographs show you what you should be aiming for at that stage in the process.

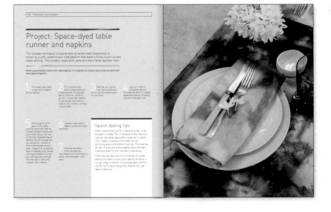

COLOUR AND PATTERN VARIATIONS
Alongside each technique there are three examples of inspirational variations in colour and pattern, which can be achieved by altering the main process slightly.

PROJECTS
Step-by-step text is given here so that you can create beautiful items for yourself or your home. Useful tips are also featured to help you achieve the best result.

HEALTH AND SAFETY INFORMATION

It is very important that, when dealing with the harsh chemicals and dyes involved with tie-dye, you observe proper health and safety protocols:

- Your workspace should be in a well-ventilated area.
- Never breathe in powdered dyes or steam from any chemicals. Always wear a paper mask when dealing with dyes and you may wish to use a respirator when doing any discharging. It is best practice to bleach items outdoors.
- Do not stand over boiling pots, and use rubber gloves and an apron at all times to protect your skin.
- Keep a wet towel close at hand to quickly wipe up any spills or accidents.

It all starts with a piece of cloth and the desire to create: when you're talking tie-dye, the possibilities are endless. There is little that can go wrong and so many possibilities to explore – basic folding in one direction gets one result; fold in another and the result will be completely different. There is always a new pleat to try or a new fabric to play with, and unravelling your tied, dipped and dyed piece is like Christmas every time.

Why we love tie-dye

Our own journey with shibori and tie-dye began more than eight years ago. We are all about simplifying traditional techniques, oversizing designs, modifying chemicals, experimenting with fabrics and celebrating the beauty of the imperfect.

Our love of dyeing has led us to work on some extreme projects. Never in our wildest dreams would we believe we would dip-dye a life-size hot air balloon or hand-dye fabric for Malibu surfboards. It's such a thrill when our work is used in the interiors of some of Australia's hottest night spots and commercial spaces, or we see our work on fashion runways.

We hope this book inspires you to think outside the box, unlock your creativity and bring out your inner child. We hope, like us, you catch the tie-dye bug, where everything you see is a potential resist and every pattern is something that can be reproduced.

Happy dyeing!

Pepa & Karen

Pepa Martin (left) and Karen Davis (right) in their studio in Sydney, Australia.

Chapter 1

Getting started

The world of tie-dye and shibori is a great way to unlock creativity you never knew you had. While we strongly advise you to experiment with as many different fabrics, ideas and techniques as possible, there are some basic principles of selecting dyes, fabrics and tools as well as health and safety procedures that you need to observe. They will save you from any 'dye-tastrophes' and allow you to achieve the best results you can.

Choosing fabrics

There are many factors that must be considered when choosing fabrics, including the fibre type, possible coating, washing process, fabric weight and surface texture or weave.

If you already have a piece of fabric that you want to dye, this will guide your technique, as some methods will be more appropriate than others for that particular fabric. For example, linen lends itself well to bold shape-resist techniques and can leave beautiful bleed lines, while lightweight cotton voile with its tight weave is perfect for stich resist. Similarly, if you start with a technique that you want to try, this will determine the fabric types that can be used, as some will offer better outcomes. If you have a purpose, such as creating a cushion cover, this will suggest the possible fabrics and the techniques.

Certain dyes are suitable for certain fabrics and will yield the best results. You may still achieve an acceptable outcome with different dyes, but you may not get the same colourfastness or intensity. More information can be found in 'Selecting dyes and recipes' (see pages 16–19).

Natural vs. synthetic fabrics
There are three types of fibres: cellulose, which is a natural fibre and includes cotton, linen, rayon and hemp; protein, which is an animal fibre and includes fabrics such as silk and wool; and man-made fibres, including synthetic fibres such as polyester, spandex, nylon and acrylic. The dyer also needs to be aware of blends; if there is a synthetic component in a cellulose or protein fibre, this will affect the outcome.

There is a time and place for synthetic fabrics, and the opportunities that they offer go hand in hand with contemporary technology and pushing the boundaries of shibori (Japanese tie-dye). For example, polyester fabric works best when using heat-set techniques due to its thermoplastic nature. However, the hand-crafted element will always complement fabrics that are natural. These fibres accept most dyes, get better results and are overwhelmingly more beautiful to touch and work with.

Fabric weight
Due to the nature of shibori, it's somewhat easier to begin with lightweight fabrics such as cotton voile, silks and muslin. Less effort may be required to manipulate these more manageable fabrics in certain techniques, and dye will penetrate thin materials more quickly. These are the fabrics that have been traditionally used in Japan. On the other hand, while dye may take longer to soak into thicker or heavier fabrics, it may be more suitable for your desired application, such as upholstery or heavy curtain fabric. The size of your

Pre-soaking

It is recommended that you pre-soak your fabric before dyeing to ensure even dye penetration. Since cloth can shrink once wet, it is possible that the resists you have applied tightly will become loose and therefore not be able to fulfill their role in resisting dye. Pre-soaking minimises this risk. Also, water acts as a temporary barrier for your dye that forces it to soak up slowly, which means it is less likely to penetrate the area that is supposed to resist the dye, creating stronger dye lines. Heavier fabrics will need to be soaked for longer periods of time.

piece will also be a determining factor in the resist technique chosen. Very labour-intensive techniques, such as stitch-resist patterns, may be more suitable to smaller pieces or as placement designs.

PFD fabrics
You are able to buy fabrics specifically made for printing or dyeing. These are often known as PFD fabrics (prepared for dyeing). These will have no coating on them and are often found in fabric stores. These are best for beginners, as no fabric preparation is required.

Linen (1), cotton (2), silk organza (3), cotton voile (4), hessian (5), cotton (6)

Selecting dyes and recipes

Choosing the right dye for your fabric will produce the best result. This is the part where your inner scientist has time to shine (you may not think you have it in you until you realize how exciting it is to mix colours). Be sure to test your dye on a small piece of cloth, as this will give you an indication of the final result.

The majority of dyes used in this book are fibre-reactive or acid dyes. You can achieve great results with all of the techniques using the more commonly available direct dyes, but the outcomes will be less vibrant and colourfast.

Fibre-reactive dyes

These dyes are normally used to dye fabrics made of cellulose fibres, such as cotton, linen and rayon. Fibre-reactive dyes can be used to dye silk or wool, but the colour will not be as strong. These dyes should not be used with synthetic materials, as they will not stay fixed to the fabric. A fibre-reactive dye is very easy to use and has great colourfastness. They are also known as cold-water dyes; however, it is easier to dissolve these dyes in hot water (no warmer than 40°C [105°F]), so this name is a little misleading. These dyes require soda ash in order for the dye to be fixed to the fabric. Table salt or urea is often added to aid dye penetration and help it colour evenly (the quantities you should add will be included in the manufacturer's instructions).

Direct dyes

Direct dyes are the most common form of dye available for home dyeing and can often be found at the supermarket or chemist. They are for use on cellulose fabrics but offer the least colourfastness of all dyes. Direct dyes yield the best result when used in boiling water with the addition of salt. Direct dyes often already contain soda ash, so no extra is required.

It is important that when you are laundering items that have been dyed with direct dyes, you sort and wash them with like colours and in cold water only.

Acid dyes

Acid dyes are used for protein fibres such as silk, wool and nylon. These are also known as hot-water dyes, as they must be dissolved in almost boiling water in order to be able to fix colour. When dyeing protein fibres, you will need a mildly acidic dye bath in order to fix the dye to the fibre. We use vinegar, a mild acid, to lower the pH of the dye bath. Acid dyes cannot be used with synthetic materials, as they will not react.

Synthetic dyes

Synthetic dyes are used for man-made fibres such as polyester. Be aware of fabric blends, as using fibre-reactive or acid dyes with cloth that is blended with a man-made material may give patchy results, depending on the synthetic percentage. In the case of a mixed-fibre fabric – for example, 90% polyester and 10% cotton – the fabric will need to be dyed twice: once with a polyester dye and once with a dye suitable for cotton.

Soda ash

Soda ash is also known as sodium carbonate or washing soda. It is a mild alkaline and raises the pH level of the liquid that the fabric is in. A high pH level is required in order for fibre-reactive dye to fix to fabric.

There are a number of ways to use soda ash. Sometimes, soda ash is dissolved in hot water and fabrics are pre-soaked in this solution before the dyeing process begins. This is the same process as degumming, in which the protective layer of silk organza – the sericin or silk gum – is removed, giving the fabric a smoother texture.

At other times, soda ash is mixed with a dye concentrate. It is not used with all dye types and is most commonly used with fibre-reactive dyes. Soda ash can also be used to remove colour in some techniques. Always read the manufacturer's instructions for directions. These will include information on weighing your fabric, which dictates the amount of soda ash you should use.

Soda ash is used because it is non-toxic and eco-friendly. That said, it is still a chemical and it is important to wear a mask and rubber gloves at all times to avoid breathing in vapours and to protect your skin and lungs.

Indigo dye

Indigo dye is derived from a plant and is the traditional dye used in Japanese shibori. There is natural indigo and man-made or synthetic indigo. You are more likely to produce stronger shades more quickly with synthetic indigo. Indigo is a vat dye, and the process makes you feel like an alchemist.

Your vat needs to be protected from the elements and, if treated with care, will last for several months The indigo vat will never become clear and be exhausted of colour. When the vat is in its green state, this indicates that the dye bath is reduced and is ready to dye the fabric. It will only turn from this healthy green colour to a blue colour if it has been accidentally oxidised (you want the oxidation to happen on your cloth instead).

Acid dye (1 and 2), indigo dye (3),
fibre-reactive dye (4), direct dye (5)

However, there are several factors to be taken into consideration when working with indigo. Indigo powder cannot be dissolved in water alone but must be used in conjunction with other chemicals in order to become water soluble. The blue indigo powder must undergo a chemical change in the vat to become water soluble. This makes it go green. When fabric is removed from the dye vat, the indigo oxidises and reverts to its insoluble form – turning blue. Follow the manufacturer's instructions to make up your indigo dye vat, as recipes differ.

Unlike fibre-reactive and acid dyes that penetrate into fabric, indigo dye sits on the surface. This makes it a great dye for beginners, as it gives instant results and beautiful textures. Just like your blue jeans, the colour will rub off, so be careful. Don't wash items dyed using indigo with regular clothing detergent, as the soda ash contained in it will remove more of the colour. To prevent this, wash these items with dishwashing liquid. Exposing indigo to the sun will fade the colour. It is hard to fail with indigo – the colour is vibrant and is stunning in every form. Synthetic indigo has been used in this book, as it is simpler to prepare for the uninitiated dyer.

Removing colour

You can also take colour out of cloth and, in doing so, reverse the typical dyeing process. Techniques will be followed as usual, but with a decolourant rather than dye, so that you are removing the colour from the area you would normally be dyeing. Fabrics need to be pre-dyed because of this.

There are three main chemicals that can be used to remove colour: discharge powder, bleach and soda ash. Discharge chemicals such as thiourea dioxide and sodium hydrosulphite can be made up as a bath or as a paste and applied to cloth. These chemicals work slowly and are the least harmful to the cloth of the decolourants. Silk can only be discharged in this way using sodium formaldehyde sulphoxylate. Bleach works very quickly but is incredibly harsh, and some materials, such as silk, would simply deteriorate if you used bleach with them. A bleach-stopping aid must be used to inhibit the bleach from

continuing to eat away at your cloth. The safest way to neutralise bleach (for the cloth as well as for the dyer) is by using sodium bisulphite or sodium metabisulphite. Sodium bisulphite chemically 'couples up' with the chlorine molecule, neutralising its effect. Hydrogen peroxide and vinegar should not be used as bleach-stopping agents, as they will combine with the bleach to create harmful chlorine gas. In large quantities, soda ash can also work as a decolourant. Again, this is only possible on certain fabrics and using certain dyes, such as direct dyes.

As with every other aspect of shibori, consider your materials and the outcome you desire before choosing which decolourant to utilise.

Natural dyes

Using natural dyes is a whole new world where colour can be made from what you have in the garden or kitchen. Beautiful patterns can be achieved in natural, earthy tones. However, the process of setting natural dyes sometimes requires very toxic chemicals. This type of dye requires people who love the art of science.

Dye-to-fabric ratio

It is important to clearly read your dye manufacturer's instructions to find out the amount of dye needed for the weight of fabric. If you find that your dye water stays very dark after the dyeing process, you are probably using too much dye.

Washing after dyeing

When washing fabric after dyeing, be sure to use a delicate laundry detergent free from harsh discolouring agents. This will remove any excess dye and maintain the strongest colour and protect your precious resist work. There are specialty chemicals, such as synthropal, that are available to make sure that no residual dye particles remain on your fabric. However, it is also possible to use regular dishwashing liquid as an alternative for home dyers.

Dye recipes

Throughout the book these dye recipes are referred to.

Synthetic indigo
Fill up a tub with 15 litres (4 gallons) of warm water. Sprinkle in your indigo powder and sodium hydrosulphite. Stir gently. Dissolve your soda ash in 30 ml (2 tablespoons) of hot water. Slowly add this solution to the dye vat. Leave for 15 minutes.

Acid dye
Fill up a tub with 15 litres (4 gallons) of water per 500g (17 oz) of dry fabric. Dissolve your acid dye in just enough boiling water to make a solution. Add ½ teaspoon of vinegar for every 1 litre (2 pints) of water. Stir thoroughly.

Fibre-reactive dye
Fill the tub with 2 litres (4 pints) warm water for every 100g (3½ oz) of dry fabric. Dissolve the fibre-reactive dye in just enough warm water to make a solution. Add it to your dye tub. Dissolve salt and soda ash in hot water (for every 2 litres (4 pints) of water you'll need 80g (2¾ oz) of salt and 30g (1 oz) of soda ash) and add to your tub. Stir.

Bleach neutralising solution
Add 1 tablespoon of sodium metabisulphite to 10 litres (2½ gallons) of water.

Degumming using soda ash
Dissolve 10 g (⅓ oz) of soda ash in 2 litres (4 pints) of boiling water in an old bucket.

Dye type	Material	Guidelines
Direct dye	Cotton and viscose	Dissolve dye in boiling water, soak fabric in soaking bucket for 15 minutes, wring out and add to dye tub. Dye fabric in boiling water with addition of table salt for 30 minutes. Rinse in cold water.
Acid dye	Wool	Add your pre-soaked wool to the dye pot. Bring the temperature slowly up to boiling point. Add vinegar (amounts detailed on dye packet). Stir and leave just below boiling point for 30 minutes, stirring regularly. Remove from dye pot and leave to sit for 10 minutes to cool down. Wash in warm water.
	Silk and nylon	Dissolve dye in boiling water (do not use water hotter than 85°C [185°F] when dyeing silk), bring water to boiling point, then add dye and acetic acid. Soak fabric in soaking bucket for 15 minutes before adding to dye tub. Dye for 15 to 30 minutes (leave for 45 to 60 minutes for darker shades). Rinse in cold water.
Fibre-reactive dye	Cotton, linen	Dissolve dye in warm water and, when cool, add water to dye pot. Add dissolved cooking salt to the dye pot. Soak fabric in soaking bucket for 10 minutes before adding to dye tub. Add cloth to dye tub and leave for 10 minutes. Dissolve soda ash and add to dye tub. Leave for another 60 to 90 minutes. Remove and rinse in cold water, then wash in hot water (60°C [140°F]), and rinse once more in cool water. If the final rinse water does not run clear, repeat the hot wash and cool rinse.
Indigo dye	Wool, cotton, silk, linen	Prepare your synthetic indigo vat. Leave for the time allocated on your manufacturer's instructions. Soak fabric in soaking bucket for 10 minutes. Wring out and put in vat for 15 minutes. Remove from vat without creating bubbles. Leave to oxidize for 10 minutes. Rinse until water runs clear. Wash with dishwashing liquid and rinse again.
Synthetic dye	Polyester and nylon	Fill dye tub with water and polyester dye and stir. Add fabric and dye for 30 to 60 minutes at boiling point.
Removing colour (thiourea dioxide recipe)	Linen, cotton dyed with fibre-reactive and direct dyes	Soak your pre-dyed and bound fabric in a soaking bucket of water. Dissolve 1 teaspoon of soda ash in 100 ml (3½ fl oz) of hot water in a pot large enough to hold just over 2 litres (4 pints) of water. Add 2 litres (4 pints) of water and bring to boil. Once boiled, add ¼ teaspoon of thiourea dioxide, stirring slowly as you go. Add fabric, simmer for 20 to 30 minutes. Remove and allow to cool. Wash in warm water with dishwashing liquid.
Bleaching	Hessian, denim	Pre-soak your fabric item in a bucket of water. Make up your bleach solution: 9 litres (2¼ gallons) of water to 250 ml (8¾ fl oz) of household bleach. Submerge your presoaked piece in the bleach mix and leave until you reach the desired result (approximately 2 hours). Remove from bleaching vessel and rinse thoroughly. Mix up your bleach neutralising solution: 1 tablespoon of sodium metabisulphite to 10 litres (2½ gallons) of water. Soak your piece for 2 hours, remove and re-rinse.

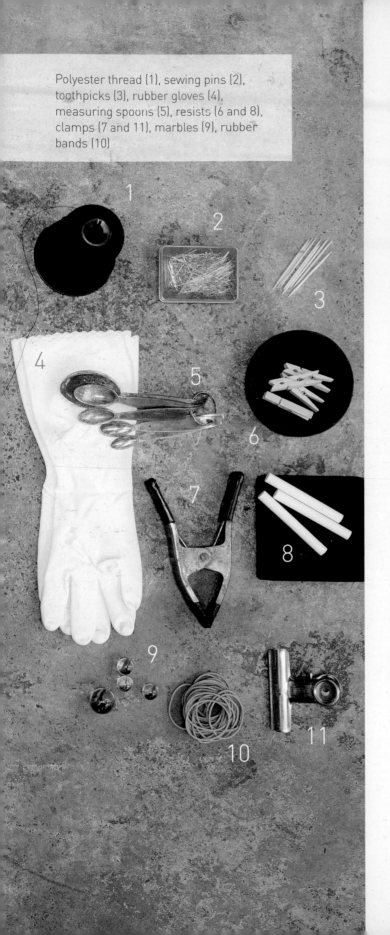

1

2

3

4

5

6

7

8

9

10

11

Selecting tools

When selecting your tools, it is important to consider their size, their capacity to fulfill their functional role and the material they are made of.

Vessels must be large enough to fit the required amount of dye and water (if necessary) as well as the entire fabric piece with space to move, potentially including resists such as poles or clamps.

Dye tubs could be large stainless-steel saucepans or plastic tubs, as these won't rust – grab any old pots or buckets that have seen better days and give them a new purpose. Plastic buckets are good for cold-water dyes, and when using techniques that require heat or the stove, you will need a metal pot. Make sure you're using non-reactive metal pots and pans, such as enamel or stainless steel. Aluminium pots will dull colours.

All tools must be able to withstand the chemicals with which they will be coming into contact. In some cases, you will be directed to use synthetic twine, as non-synthetic twine will absorb the dye and not act as a resist.

Once a tool or vessel has been used for dyeing, it must not be used for anything else again. Source an appropriate tub and label it 'Dyeing', and store all tools and chemicals within this, so that nothing is accidentally used in the kitchen or elsewhere in the home.

A resist item (see page 22) should be the shape and size that you desire for your pattern, and the tools (such as string or clamps) must have the strength and tension to hold these items in place. Find anything around the house and try it out. These could be any two things that are the same shape, such as old tiles, rulers, jar lids, pegs or cooking utensils. You should not need to buy anything new for these techniques. Soon you will be considering everything in your home to be a potential resist!

While shibori is a super-fun activity, don't forget that you're working with hazardous chemicals and you should always exercise good practice when it comes to health and safety. See page 9 for more information on working safely.

Plumber's pipe (1), saucepan (2),
ruler (3), rope (4), scissors (5),
heavy plastic twine (6), bamboo
steamer (7)

Folding and clamping fabric

There are so many ways to translate shibori onto your cloth. You have the power to plan your design, and there is nothing stopping you from thinking outside the box – but it is important to consider basic design elements. This involves playing with scale, direction and tone.

There are so many exciting techniques and colours to try, and often the hardest thing to do is to keep it simple. It is a good idea to record your shibori process through photos and a visual diary, so that you will always remember how to create a pattern.

The concept of planning a design comes down to the resist technique you are using: this is the way you fold and hold your fabric together before it is dyed. Pleats are about folding cloth in certain ways and securing them to create a resist. The folds stop dye from penetrating through the entire cloth and remain undyed, the pleat forms the repeat, and the consequence is a beautiful shibori pattern. The way in which the pleat is held, whether it is with clamps or string, will add to the design and allow for further variations. No matter how simple or complex, every fold has the power to create a story on your cloth.

Appreciate positive and negative space – the areas that are not dyed are just as important as those that are. They may offer a moment of serenity in untouched, white cloth that works to highlight a simple, beautiful strip of shibori on one end. You may wish to cover the whole piece in a repeat pattern, or discharge a design into already coloured fabric. In this way, placement is essential and has the power to transform the mood of your final piece.

Considering space and placement in your design plan could include dyeing an area that is off-centre, altering your symmetry and playing with size. All of these things are what makes a piece of hand-dyed cloth truly your own creation.

Shibori uses a series of pleats to create organised repeats. The pleat can be used to create different effects or textures within your resists. One of the most common pleats used in shibori is the accordion pleat. Folding the fabric back and forth in an 'accordion' or 'concertina'-like manner ensures that the fabric is always on the outside as opposed to rolling in on itself, which buries the inner layers. Another pleat to experiment with is step pleats, in which the fabric is pleated in one direction and the pleats sit next to each other with space in between. This space is your exposed area, which, when bound, will display your pattern, and the hidden step forms a dye barrier or another level of resistance. Pleating is another way to add a sophisticated repeat to your shibori experience. Combining pleating with stitching takes your design to a whole new level, and experimenting further with pleats will offer you unlimited possibilities.

ACCORDION PLEATS

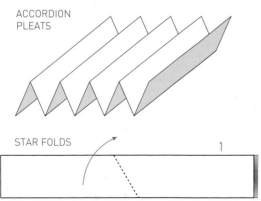

STAR FOLDS

1

To create your star folds, you must, first, accordion pleat your fabric. Fold your length of fabric, beginning in the center at the angle shown above.

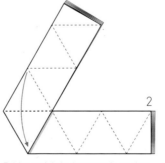

2

Fold your fabric downwards so that you are creating equilateral triangles as you fold.

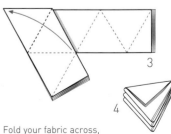

3

4

Fold your fabric across, continuing to create equilateral triangles until you are left with a triangular stack.

Household clothes pegs (1), plastic twine (2), resist shapes (3), rubber band (4)

Heat-set pleats on polyester fabric (1), bound fabric on mixed fibres (2), bound fabric on cotton (3)

Colour

Colour wheels, palettes and mood boards are wonderful tools, but when it comes down to it, colour is subjective and your aesthetic will determine what you are attracted to. As artists, we tend to move towards tertiary and moody colours because, to us, they create subtle pieces that echo the way in which they were created – by hand.

Drawing designs and noting colour schemes are a great way of working up ideas before committing material and dyes.

Bright, rich colours are often associated with tie-dye, and these might be the tones that make your heart soar. But there is always more to the colour than simply the colour choice itself. If you are utilising the ombré technique, there will be a gradation of the same colour, and in the scrunch technique, a vast array of different tones will be revealed. Most techniques will provide a number of tones due to the perfect inconsistencies of hand dyeing. Over time, you will have the skill to manipulate the strength of the tone and mix colours so that you are more likely to get exactly what you want. With practice and confidence, most aspects of shibori can be played with, manipulated and adapted.

It is important to consider the reality of bleeding dye lines. These create incredible textural aspects to a cloth, but may be disappointing if colours are placed too closely together and mix with one another. Yellow and blue dyes will give you green – all of the same colour theory rules you learned in art class apply when dyeing fabric. Think about whether this should be avoided, adapt your resists accordingly and choose colours carefully.

Don't forget that the colour of the dye powder is rarely the colour of the dye. Also, the colour will always be lighter once the piece is dry – so allow your shades to become darker during the wet dyeing process.

Consider your colour palette, the purpose of the dyed cloth and the space in which it will exist. Colour combined with pattern creates the mood of your fabric. A grey stripe might be a strong statement, whereas a grey scrunch can be soft and delicate. Think about the story that you want it to tell and choose your colour with intent.

Some basic colour theory

Primary colours are red, yellow and blue. They are colours that can't be created by mixing other colours. When they are mixed together, they create secondary colours.

Warm colours, such as red, yellow and orange, are bright and energetic. Cool colours, such as blue and green, give the impression of calm and are soothing to the eye. While warm colours tend to advance, cool colours look as if they are receding. All of these are important factors to consider when working on a design. White, black and grey are neutral shades. Neutral colours are great to use alongside strong colours in order to tone them down or can be used alone to create subtle designs.

When you are working with dyes, you will find pre-made dyes of these colours readily available to you. Often the powder form does not resemble the final dyed outcome, so it's a good idea to do test swatches of all your colours. Once you have these colours, you can experiment with mixing shades to make your own unique colour palette. It's a good idea to keep a diary of your dye recipes for future experimentation. Colour can open up a whole new world, and mixing dye colours can be just as fun as making shibori patterns.

Secondary colours are green, orange and purple. They are made up by mixing combinations of red, yellow and blue.

Red + Yellow = Orange
Yellow + Blue = Green
Blue + Red = Purple

Tertiary colours are made up from the mixing of combinations of both primary and secondary colours.

For example:
Orange + Yellow = Warm Yellow
Red + Orange = Warm Red
Red + Purple = Cool Red
Blue + Purple = Cool Blue
Blue + Green = Warm Blue
Yellow + Green = Warm Green

Each pair of linen swatches has been dyed with a fibre-reactive dye at full strength and at 35% strength.

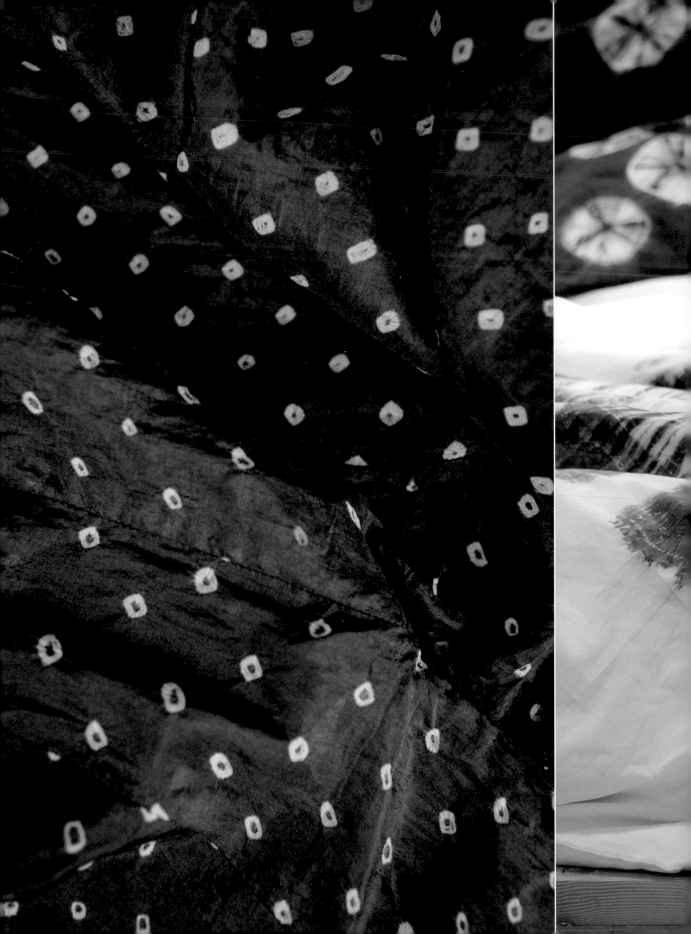

Chapter 2

Techniques and projects

The beauty of tie-dye and modern shibori is that there are endless possibilities. With a little bit of know-how and a lot of imagination, you have the ability to create something beautiful and one of a kind.

All the techniques and projects in this book have evolved from things learned, mastered and tinkered with. Every project and technique can be re-interpreted in millions of different ways, and a different outcome can be as simple as changing the fabric, dye, size or placement of your resist or stitches. There are no right or wrong outcomes, only exploration and experimentation.

While some techniques have a strong grounding in traditional Japanese shibori, others are inspired by the liberating notion of tie-dye. Feel free to mix and match, and be confident and have fun, for your tie-dye adventure begins now!

Ombré
Dip-dyeing

Dip-dye, otherwise known as ombré, is a dyeing technique in which shades of colour graduate from light to dark. Commonly used in fashion and interiors, this simple technique has the ability to add subtle sophistication to fabric. Depending on the colour used, dip-dye can appear soft and elegant, or dramatic and eye catching.

3

Dip-dyeing can be done in a multitude of ways. The artist must first decide the desired outcome for this delicate finish, as the feel can be drastically changed depending on a number of factors.

For example, the placement of the darkest tone will totally change the impact of the piece. If the darkest tone is placed at the bottom and lightens as it rises up the piece, the effect is uplifting and feminine. If the tones are reversed and the darkest tone is at the top, the opposite effect is created. If the darkest tone is placed in the middle and lightens outwards, a dramatic effect is created, emphasising an area and creating a focal point. The dark tone will attract attention and can be used as a tool depending on the purpose of the piece. In fashion, it can be used to accentuate body shape. The size of the dark tone and the range of colour will transform the fabric. Very dark with little range will create heaviness, whereas dark with an extensive range requires much attention but lightens the piece significantly. Having the darkest tone as a midtone will transform the result to be soft and subtle, whether there is an extensive range or not. Introducing multiple points of gradation, slowly moving through monochromatic tones, will give a sense of movement to a piece and can add natural texture that is far from planned.

Though dip-dyeing may seem quite a simple process, creating a seamless gradation of tone is much harder than it first appears. The fabric must constantly be lifted up and down so that no clear banding lines appear. Successful dip-dyeing requires precision and patience, but is well worth the effort.

4

you will need

White or lightly coloured cotton fabric (1)

Soaking bucket

Dye tub (2)

Rubber gloves

Paper mask

Direct dye (3)

Three glass jars (4)

Coat hanger with a horizontal bar or a piece of dowel

How to create a gradated dip-dye

1 Soak the piece of fabric in a bucket of water for 15 minutes. Remove the fabric from the bucket, wringing out the excess water, then fill the dye tub with warm water.

2 Dissolve the direct dye in 500 ml (1 pint) of warm water. Distribute the dye concentrate equally into three jars. The dye in the jars is all the same concentration and is diluted when poured into the dye bath. The principle of submersion dyeing is that the dye is used up when the water has run clear. This method works by layering the colour so that the bottom layer will have all three levels, hence the darker pigmentation.

Pour one jar of dye into the water in the dye tub.

3 Hang the top of the fabric from a coat hanger or dowel. This area will remain white and therefore will not be entering the dye bath.

4 Submerge three-quarters of the fabric in the dye bath. Leave for 20 minutes, agitating regularly.

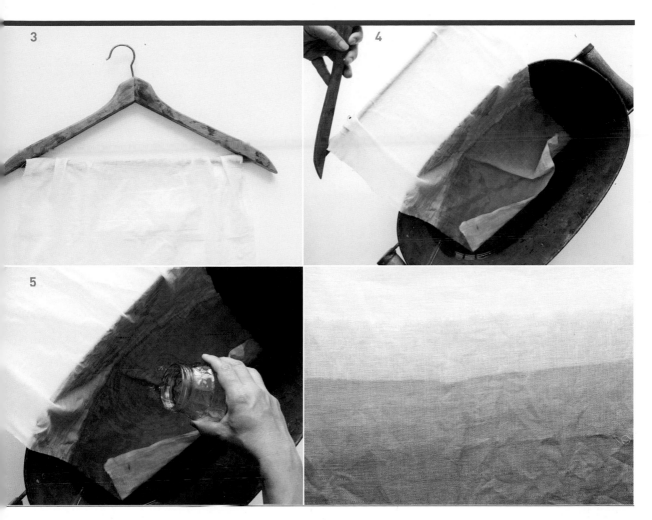

5 Raise one-quarter of the fabric out of the dye bath. It may be easier to suspend the hanger from a chair or low table. Pour in the second jar of dye, ensuring that you do not pour directly onto the fabric. Leave for 20 minutes, agitating regularly.

6 Lift the fabric again, leaving only the bottom quarter in the dye bath.

7 Pour in the third jar of dye concentrate, ensuring that you do not pour it directly onto the fabric. Leave for 20 minutes, agitating regularly.

8 Carefully remove your fabric from the dye bath. It is important not to mark the white areas with dye. Rinse with cold water running away from the white section. Rinse until the water runs clear.

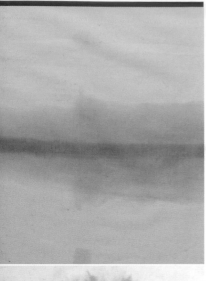

1 Stripes

Adding ombré effects gives dimension to basic stripes.

Iron your cloth and accordion pleat it as if you were creating basic stripes (see page 48). The pleat defines the size of your stripe. Hold your pleats together with clamps and place the fabric in a soaking bucket for 10 minutes. Fill your dye tub with 1 litre (2 pints) of warm water. Prepare your fibre-reactive dye as per the instructions on page 18. Pour approximately 2 cm (¾ inch) of the dye into the dye tub. This will be your darkest section of stripe.

Remove the cloth from the bucket and dab the excess water with a towel. Holding the clamps, drape the edge of your pleats into the dye tub and leave for 15 minutes. Then add warm water to the dye tub to lift the water level an extra 5 cm (2 inches) and leave for 15 minutes. This will dilute your dye and give you a lighter shade. If you wish, you can add smaller amounts of water and increase the level of gradation. Refer to the instructions for the total dye time required to ensure each colour level has time to set. Once the dye process is complete, remove the fabric without getting the white area in the dye, rinse, remove the clamps and rinse again.

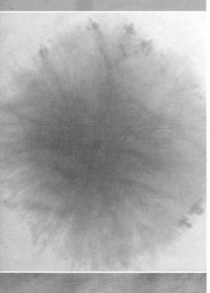

2 Circle

By isolating an area on your fabric, you can create a dip-dye focal point.

Lay your fabric on a flat surface. Using your thumb and index finger, pinch the centre of your fabric into a peak. Maintaining the pinch, run your other hand down the fabric and then stop at the desired size of your dip-dye circle. Place a rubber band at this point to secure.

Soak this area to just above the rubber band for 10 minutes. Wring out. Fill a small dye tub with 2 litres (4 pints) of water per 100 g (3½ oz) of dry fabric. Prepare your fibre-reactive dye as per the instructions on page 18.

Holding the fabric securely at the base of the rubber band, submerge your full gathered circle. Leave for 2 minutes or until there is a light shade of colour. Raise one-quarter of the dipped fabric and leave for 10 minutes. Raise another quarter and leave for another 20 minutes or until the water is colourless (this will give you the darkest shade possible). This is known as exhausting the dye tub.

3 Two ends

Dip-dyeing from the top and bottom accentuates the centre of the fabric.

Fold your fabric in half and place in a soaking bucket for 10 minutes. Fill your dye tub with 1 litre (2 pints) of warm water. Prepare your fibre-reactive dye as per the instructions on page 18. Remove your fabric from the soaking bucket and wipe off the excess water with a towel.

Drape the fabric over a hanger so that both sides are equally aligned. Fill your dye tub with approximately 10 cm (4 inches) of warm water and stir in the dye concentrate. Lower the hanger so that the ends of your fabric are submerged (this will be the darkest shade). Move the fabric to spread the dye evenly, being careful not to splash the white area. Leave for 15 to 20 minutes. Add warm water, raising the water level an extra 5 to 10 cm (2 to 4 inches). This will dilute the dye concentrate and give the lighter shade. Agitate the fabric to spread the dye evenly.

Once the dye process is complete, carefully remove the fabric. Rinse until the water runs clear and leave on the hanger to dry to ensure that your white stays white!

Project: Dip-dye summer dress

Dip-dye (or ombré) is a great way to embellish your favourite summer dress. Adding simple colour gradation is elegant, individual and a great way to turn an everyday dress into a one-of-a-kind garment.

Remember: When dip-dyeing, it is important to keep the area of the dress you would like to remain white out of the way of the dye to avoid marks or spills.

1 Place your cotton dress in a soaking bucket for 15 to 30 minutes. Prepare your fibre-reactive dye by dissolving it in just enough warm water to make a solution.

2 Remove your dress from the soaking bucket and wring out. Place the dress on a coat hanger.

3 Fill your dye tub with approximately 25 cm (10 inches) of warm water and stir in the dye concentrate. Lower the dress so that the bottom third is submerged (this will be the darkest shade). Move the dress to spread the dye evenly, being careful not to splash the white area. Dissolve salt in hot water and add to the dye bath. Dissolve soda ash in hot water and add to the dye bath (see fibre-reactive recipe on page 18 for guidance on amounts). Leave for 15 to 20 minutes, agitating regularly.

4 Add warm water, raising the water level an extra 25 cm (10 inches) or as high as you would like the ombré effect. This will dilute the dye concentrate and give a lighter shade. Agitate the fabric to spread the dye evenly.

5 After another 20 minutes, carefully remove the dress from the dye tub. Rinse until the water runs clear and leave on the hanger while drying to ensure your white stays white!

Dip-dye tips

Fibre-reactive dyes work best on cotton and linen fabrics. If your dress is made out of silk or wool, follow these steps using acid dye.

Deciding the best area to dip-dye depends on your dress. For a long maxi dress, you may decide to highlight the length by dip-dyeing only the bottom; however, it might be interesting to dye the mid-section as a feature.

5

7

1

Arashi Pole wrapping

'Arashi' is the Japanese word for storm – the traditional version of this technique resembles heavy rain in a storm. The playful nature of arashi opens the imagination to the countless possibilities of tie-dye.

Arashi uses a long pole and fabric compression to form a resist that leaves stripes on the fabric. The fabric is wrapped around the pole in a specific way (in order to achieve the desired pattern), fixed in place with rubber bands and squashed as far as possible to one end of the pole. The pole is then submerged in a dye bath. Wrapping the fabric in different ways will produce different patterns.

The traditional form of arashi involves wrapping the fabric at a 45-degree angle to the pole, creating a diagonal stripe. There have been many modifications to modernise this technique that vary the size, direction and scale of the stripes, according to the way the fabric is wrapped around the pole, the angle at which it is wrapped, whether the fabric is pleated before wrapping and much more.

The beauty of arashi is in its movement. It portrays impressions of water, such as a choppy ocean or stormy sky, and the powerful emotions that these images evoke. The patterns are striking, organised but organic in design and with an element of the unknown that is always in play when working with shibori.

By far one of the most fascinating techniques, arashi shows that the world of dyeing has much to offer.

2

3

6

4

---

you will need

Iron

Strip of white or lightly coloured cotton approximately 30 cm (12 inches) wide (1)

NOTE: The size of your fabric is determined by the diameter of your plastic plumbing pipe. If you want to dye a larger piece of fabric, you will need a wider pole.

Approximately 50 cm (20 inches) of plastic plumbing pipe 10 cm (4 inches) in diameter (2)

Rubber bands (3)

Soaking bucket

Towel

Paper mask

Rubber gloves (4)

Dye vat large enough to submerge your plumbing pipe

Spoon (5)

Indigo dye (6)

Small scissors (7)

Sodium hydrosulphite

Soda ash

How to tie-dye using pole wrapping

1 Iron the piece of fabric, then lay it down on a hard surface.

2 Place the plumbing pipe diagonally on top of the fabric, with one end of the pole positioned in the top corner. Wrap the fabric over the pole, ensuring that the two edges of fabric meet up but do not overlap. Any overlapping fabric will cause a ghosting or masked-out effect on your pattern.

3 Secure the fabric around both ends of the pipe with rubber bands.

4 Wrap rubber bands around the pipe at approximately 2-cm (¾-inch) intervals. Make sure they are tight enough to resist the dye and double over if necessary.

5 Push the fabric down hard to compress the fabric between the bands. This compression is what creates your resist.

6 Soak the pipe in a bucket of water for 15 minutes. Remove the pipe from the water and dab the excess water with a towel.

7 Prepare your synthetic indigo vat by filling up a tub with 15 litres (4 gallons) of warm water. Sprinkle in your indigo powder and sodium hydrosulphite. Stir gently. Dissolve your soda ash in 30 ml (2 tablespoons) of hot water. Slowly add this solution to the dye vat. Leave for 30 minutes. Submerge the wrapped pipe in the dye vat and leave for 15 minutes; do not agitate.

8 Rinse under cold water until the water runs clear. Remove the rubber bands from the pipe; sometimes it's easier and more time-effective to cut the bands off using small scissors. Rinse the fabric again until the water runs clear.

1 Degum

Degumming silk organza adds an opaque effect to a sheer material.

Lay your fabric on a flat surface and iron out any creases. Accordion pleat it at approximately 7.5-cm (3-inches) intervals. Place your strip of pleated fabric horizontally on the table and place the plumbing pipe diagonally across the fabric. Roll the fabric diagonally along the pipe and secure both ends with rubber bands.

Place rubber bands down the length of the pipe, compressing the fabric as you go. Place the fabric in a soaking bucket for 20 minutes. Remove and squeeze out the water.

Prepare your soda ash solution as per the instructions on page 18. Submerge the silk on the plumbing pipe into your hot soda ash solution. Leave for 30 minutes.

Remove the pipe from the dye vat and rinse under cold water. Release the silk from the pipe. Add 2 tablespoons of white vinegar to a bucket of water and neutralise the silk for 10 minutes. Wring out and hang out to dry.

2 Straight

Using arashi on a horizontal line instead of a diagonal creates the feel of a calm ocean rather than a storm.

Lay your fabric on a flat surface and iron out any creases. Roll your fabric straight around the plumbing pipe and secure both ends with rubber bands.

Place rubber bands down the length of the pipe, compressing the fabric as you go. Place the fabric in a soaking bucket for 20 minutes. Prepare your synthetic indigo vat as per the instructions on page 18. Remove the pipe from the soaking bucket and wring out the excess water. Submerge the wrapped pipe in the dye vat and leave for 15 minutes; do not agitate.

Remove the pipe from the dye vat and allow it to oxidise for 15 minutes. Rinse under cold water. Then release the fabric from the pipe and rinse until the water runs clear.

3 Chevron

A textural and random V-shaped pattern that produces unexpected results when using arashi.

Lay your fabric on a flat surface and iron out any creases. Accordion pleat your fabric at approximately 7.5-cm (3-inch) intervals. Place your strip of pleated fabric horizontally on the table and place the plumbing pipe diagonally across the fabric. Roll the fabric diagonally along the pipe and secure both ends with rubber bands.

Place rubber bands down the length of the pipe, compressing the fabric down as you go. Place the fabric in a soaking bucket for 20 minutes. Prepare your synthetic indigo vat as per the instructions on page 18. Remove the pipe from the soaking bucket and wring out the excess water. Submerge the wrapped pipe in the dye vat and leave for 30 minutes; do not agitate.

Remove the pipe from the dye vat and allow it to oxidise for 15 minutes. Rinse under cold water. Then release the fabric from the pipe and rinse under cold water.

1

2

3

Project: Arashi tote bag

The beautiful feathery lines of arashi are a great texture to dress up your tote or shopping bag.

If you are using a calico shopping or tote bag, it's a good idea to soak it in boiling water to remove the coating that is commonly found on the fabric.

1 Pre-wash your tote bag to create a good base for dyeing.

2 Lay your tote bag on a flat surface and iron out the creases.

3 Place your plumbing pipe diagonally across the cloth bag. Roll your bag around the pipe and secure both ends with rubber bands.

4 Wrap rubber bands around the pipe at approximately 2.5-cm (1-inch) intervals, compressing the bag as you go. Make sure they are tight enough to resist the dye, and double over if necessary. Include the handles to give an all-over finish.

5 Place the bound pipe in a soaking bucket for 30 minutes.

6 Remove the pipe from the water, squeeze out the excess water and dab with a towel.

7 Prepare your synthetic indigo vat by filling up a tub with 15 litres (4 gallons) of warm water. Sprinkle in your indigo powder and sodium hydrosulphite. Stir gently. Dissolve your soda ash in 30 ml (2 tablespoons) of hot water. Slowly add this solution to the dye vat. Leave for 30 minutes. Submerge the wrapped pipe in the dye vat and leave for 40 minutes; do not agitate as this will create bubbles.

8 Remove the pipe from the dye vat and leave to oxidise for 15 minutes. Rinse under cold water until the water runs clear. Then release the fabric from the pipe, rinse again and wash with dishwashing liquid until the water runs clear.

Contemporary arashi

In traditional Japanese arashi, the shibori artist uses a wooden pole instead of a plumbing pipe – as a result, this technique is often referred to as pole wrapping. Contemporary American artists were the first to use discarded plumbing pipes in shibori. The Americans also introduced bright, clashing colours and the random placement of designs on fabric, which became a well-known symbol of the Swinging Sixties.

Mokume
Textured stitching

Mokume is a Japanese shibori stitch technique known for its woodgrain-like textural pattern. This resist involves stitching with a needle and thread in rows of parallel running stitches. The threads are then pulled tightly, bringing the fabric together and creating gathered areas that the dye cannot penetrate. It is the most simple of the stitch resists and is a good introduction to more advanced techniques.

Stitching techniques are more advanced than dip-, space or scrunch dyeing techniques. They require precision and the planning of a design. There are many different types of stitching techniques used throughout Japan that change the effect on the fabric. Often these stitches are combined on the same piece to highlight different areas and form a resist illustration. For example, mokume may be used with more advanced stitching techniques such as maki-nui and karamatsu shibori.

Despite the basic nature of mokume, there are quite a few things to remember in order to achieve the best possible result. Using a ruler and tailor's chalk allows you to map out and track where your stitches will be placed. It is also a good idea to use contrasting thread to highlight your stitched area. Experiment with small test pieces of fabric in order to understand the exact amount of tension required when pulling the threads and gathering the fabric together.

Mokume opens the door to an entire library of stitches and the possibilities that come with them. It is easy to use stitches to illustrate basic shapes, and the technique allows the artist to make more complex dyed placement prints.

3

you will need

Iron

Cotton or natural
dyed fabric (1)

Tailor's chalk

Ruler

Sewing needle and
thread (2)

Soaking bucket

Towel

Paper mask

Rubber gloves (3)

Dye pot

Acid dye (4)

Scissors (5)

Vinegar

Stitch ideas

Decorative stitching can also
be used to embellish finished
pieces. A Japanese craft called
sashiko traditionally goes hand in
hand with mokume.

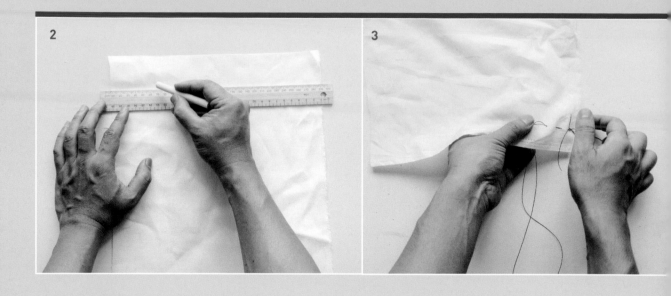

Using textured stitching

1 Iron the piece of fabric, then lay it down on a hard surface.

2 Using tailor's chalk and a ruler, draw horizontal lines on your fabric 2 cm (¾ inch) apart.

3 Double-thread the needle and tie it off with a strong knot. Sew along the first line with running stitch. When you reach the end, cut the thread to a length of 15 cm (6 inches). Secure the end with a knot. (You will use this thread to pull all the stitches together on the line you have just sewn.)

4 Repeat the process until all your ruled lines are stitched.

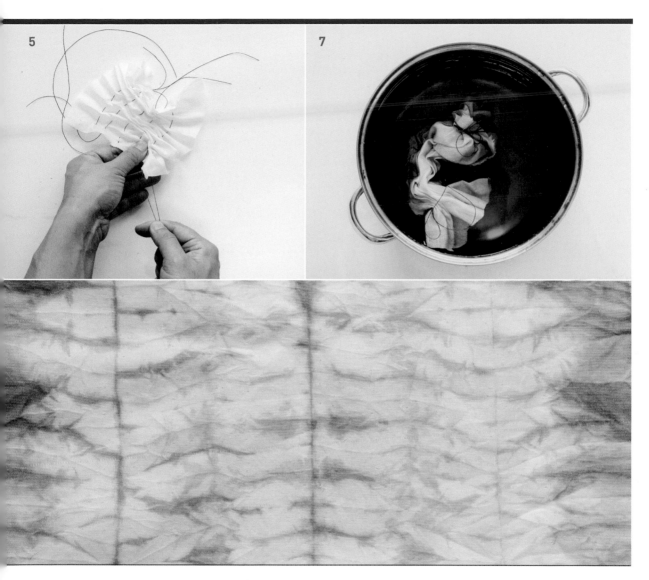

5 Collect all the ends of thread together from each row, and gently pull then push the fabric with your other hand, creating a gathered effect. Secure the pulled threads with a tight knot.

6 Soak the fabric in a bucket of water for 15 minutes. Remove from the water and dab the excess water with a towel.

7 Fill the dye pot with 10 litres (2½ gallons) warm water per 500 g (17 oz) of dry fabric. Prepare your acid dye by dissolving it in boiling water. Add vinegar. Place the fabric into the dye pot, ensuring it is submerged. Leave to dye in the simmering pot for 30 minutes, agitating regularly.

8 Once the dye process is complete, rinse under warm running water, then cut the knots and remove the stitches. Rinse again until the water runs clear.

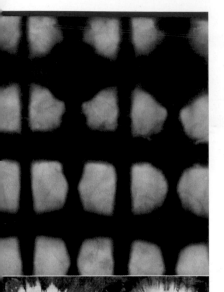

1 Boxes

Here, you are using a very simple, very effective, traditional technique.

Iron your fabric. Starting from the end, fold the fabric forwards 5 cm (2 inches), and then fold this forwards twice more (maintaining the same width) in order to create four levels of fabric that are 5 cm (2 inches), with the excess fabric coming out of the side. Iron flat. Turn your piece to the side and accordion pleat the folded fabric. Using a double-threaded needle, pass the needle through your accordion pleats in order to make the gather hold. Knot the thread to secure.

Place the fabric in a soaking bucket for 20 minutes. Prepare your synthetic indigo vat as per the instructions on page 18. Remove the bound fabric from the soaking bucket and wring out the excess water. Submerge the fabric in the dye vat and leave for 15 minutes; do not agitate.

When complete, remove from the dye vat and allow it to oxidise for 15 minutes. Rinse the fabric under cold water until the water runs clear before undoing the stitches and exposing a box pattern.

2 Heart

Illustrate your shibori by creating basic shapes with stitch resist.

Fold your fabric in half and iron. Using tailor's chalk, draw half a heart, using the fold as the centre. Prepare a needle with double thread and knot at the end. Beginning at the top of your folded heart, follow your line with a running stitch, gathering as you go. When you reach the end of the heart, pull the threads as tightly as possible and tie a tight knot.

Place the fabric in a soaking bucket for 10 to 15 minutes. Remember, when your fabric is wet, you may be able to tighten the stitches further due to the fabric shrinkage. Prepare your synthetic indigo vat as per the instructions on page 18. Remove your fabric from the soaking bucket and submerge the entire cloth in the dye vat for 15 minutes.

When complete, remove the fabric and allow it to oxidise for 15 minutes. Rinse under cold water until the water runs clear before undoing your stitches.

3 Stripes

This classic stripe design can be re-invented in so many ways – including textural.

Fold your fabric in half. Using a double-threaded needle, work running stitches along the length of your fold, gathering tightly as you go. When you reach the end, wind the thread tightly around your gathered stitched line. Then continue to wind the thread tightly down the length of the fabric for an extra 20 cm (8 inches), creating a bound tube. Spread the fabric out at this point and repeat the running stitch to form the stitched gathered line as you did originally. Wind the thread again and repeat until all fabric is bound.

Place the fabric in a soaking bucket for 20 minutes. Prepare your fibre-reactive dye as per the instructions on page 18. Remove from the soaking bucket and wring out the excess water. Submerge the fabric in the dye vat and leave for 30 minutes, agitating regularly to ensure that it is dyed evenly. Remove from the dye vat and rinse under cold water until the water runs clear, then undo the stitches.

Project: Silk-stitch shibori head scarf

A great way to show off your shibori stitch skills is to transform an old silk head scarf into a beautiful accessory sure to win compliments.

When first practising stitch shibori, it is good to start with a smaller piece and use a contrasting thread so that you can see your stitches clearly. Experiment with the tension and make sure the threads are pulled tight after pre-soaking to ensure you get a positive result.

1 Lay your silk scarf on a flat surface and iron.

2 Starting from one end, fold the fabric forwards 5 cm (2 inches) and then fold this forwards twice more (maintaining the same width) in order to create four levels of fabric that are 5 cm (2 inches), with the excess fabric coming out of the side. Iron flat.

3 Turn your piece to the side by 90 degrees and accordion pleat the folded fabric. Using a double-threaded needle, sew through the accordion pleats, using a running stitch in order to make the gather hold. Knot the thread to secure.

4 Soak the scarf in a bucket of water for 20 minutes. Remove from the water and dab the excess water with a towel.

5 Fill a stainless steel or enamel dye pot with 15 litres (4 gallons) warm water per 500 g (17 oz) of dry fabric. Prepare the acid dye by dissolving it in just enough hot water to make a solution, and add to the dye pot. Bring the water in the dye pot to a boil. Place the scarf in the dye pot and leave for 10 minutes, agitating regularly to ensure it is evenly dyed. Add 2 tablespoons of vinegar

6 Once the dye process is complete, rinse under cold running water, then cut the knots and remove the stitches. Rinse again until the water runs clear.

Dyeing silk

It is recommended that you use acid dye with silk to get the most intense colour. While direct dyes or fibre-reactive dyes will give some colour, the results will not be as vibrant as the colour you anticipate. Soda ash will also have an effect on your silk and remove the sheen.

Silk habotai, also known as China silk, is a lightweight silk commonly used for scarves. It has a plain weave and is often used by artists to paint on and embellish. It is sturdy enough to manipulate with stitches and has a beautiful lustre, so it would work well with this technique.

Cotton voile is a good alternative to silk. It has similar properties and dyes well with fibre-reactive dye, indigo or direct dyes.

Kumo Spider-web binding

'Kumo' – meaning spider in Japanese – creates patterns that resemble the fine lines of a spider's web. This technique can be realised in many surprising and unexpected ways, the most popular being the tie-dye or hippie circles that made these dyeing techniques household patterns.

Kumo is made up of a series of circles placed within one another, from large to small, that seem to be joined together by the imprints of the bind lines. The basic principle of kumo is to pull a peak in the fabric and bind fine thread from the bottom of the area that has been peaked, to the top, and back down to the bottom. This creates a sausage shape of bound fabric. At its base, the rest of the fabric spreads out and the process is repeated, depending on how many web-like patterns you wish to see on the final piece. The pattern can be transformed by altering the size of each bound circle or varying the spacing between the binding.

Traditionally, a hook or similar tool is used to create the peak so that both hands are free to bind. In order to make the binding process easier for beginners, it is a good idea to insert a toothpick or similar object into the peak in order to hold it in place and create a firm base on which to bind.

Kumo works especially well on a silk dupioni or similar silk with a tight weave. The natural slub found in silk adds extra spider-like textures, and the tightly woven fibres emphasise the delicate lines of the web. This technique is commonly seen detailing vintage kimonos and is one of the more recognisable Japanese shibori techniques.

you will need

Iron

Piece of white or lightly coloured silk (1)

Toothpicks (2)

Polyester or nylon thread (3)

Small scissors (4)

Soaking bucket

Towel

Paper mask

Rubber gloves (5)

Dye tub

Wooden spoon (6)

Acid dye (7)

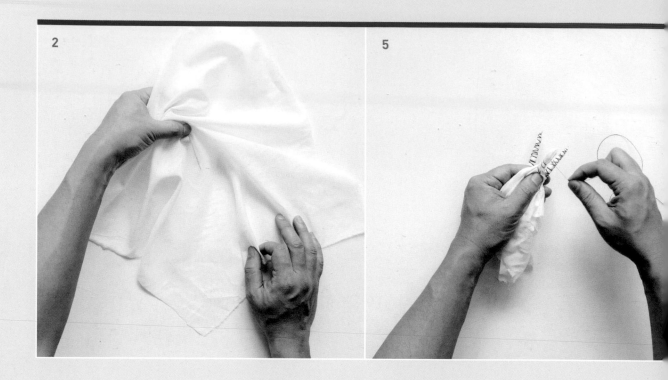

How to bind and dye a spider-web pattern

1 Iron your piece of silk.

2 Create a peak by positioning a toothpick underneath the fabric.

3 Wrap the fabric around the toothpick to create little pleats.

4 Holding the base of the toothpick and the thread, bind the thread from the base of the peak to the top and back down. Secure the thread with a knot and cut the end.

7

5 Repeat until you have a cluster of bound toothpicks.

6 Soak the fabric in a bucket of water for 20 minutes. Remove the fabric from the water and dab the excess water with a towel.

7 Prepare your fibre-reactive dye by dissolving it in just enough warm water to make a solution. Boil 2 litres (4 pints) of water and add your dye solution to it. Place the fabric in the dye, ensuring that it is submerged. Leave for 30 minutes, agitating regularly.

8 Rinse under cold running water, remove the binding and toothpicks from the fabric and rinse the fabric again until the water runs clear.

1 Heat set

The beautiful peaks of heat-set kumo add an incredible tactile element to cloth.

This technique is often used on silk; however, washing will destroy the kumo impressions. To avoid this, use heat-set synthetic fabric that will maintain its shape after washing. Dampen the synthetic fabric with a spray bottle of water. Create a small peak from the underside of the fabric. Pinch the top of this peak and bind from the base to the top and back down again with thread, tying off securely. Repeat until you reach the desired number of peaks.

Wrap the bound piece in newspaper or muslin to protect it. Place in your bamboo steamer. Fill your wok with a little boiling water, place the bamboo steamer in the wok, and steam for 20 minutes. When cooled, remove the fabric from the steamer, unwrap it, and test by undoing a bound peak. If you are happy with the heat-set piece, continue to remove the thread. If your fabric is thick or very large, it may require another 10 minutes of steaming. Re-bind the test peak and continue to steam. Your piece is now finished, and washing in cold water is optional.

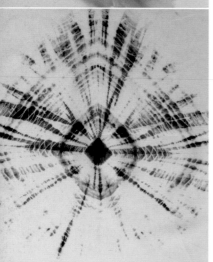

2 Large

Playing with scale highlights the delicate webbed lines of kumo.

Lay your fabric on a flat surface. Using your thumb and index finger, pinch the centre of your fabric to the desired size of your kumo circle. Place a rubber band at the base to secure. Dampen your gathered circle to just above the rubber band. Using synthetic thread, wind from the base of the circle to the tip and back down again, then tie off.

Place the fabric in a soaking bucket for 10 minutes. Prepare your synthetic indigo vat as per the instructions on page 18. Remove the fabric from the soaking bucket and wring out the excess water. Holding the fabric securely at the base of the rubber band, submerge the entire gathered circle in your dye vat for 10 minutes (you may have to hold it or drape it over the side).

Remove the fabric and be careful not to splash the white areas and allow it to oxidise for 15 minutes. Rinse with cold water running away from the white section until the water runs clear.

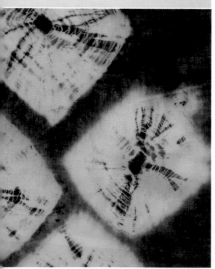

3 Two-colour dyes

This creates delicate kumo circles on a hand-dyed block colour background.

Lay your fabric flat and pinch the fabric to the desired size of your circle. Place a rubber band at the base. Dampen your gathered circle to just above the rubber band. Using synthetic thread, wind from the base to the tip and back down again, then tie off. Bind more circles as desired.

Soak your fabric for 10 minutes. Prepare your synthetic indigo vat as per the instructions on page 18. Remove the fabric from the soaking bucket and wring out the excess water. Holding the fabric securely at the base of all the rubber bands, submerge only the gathered circles in your dye vat for 10 minutes.

Remove your fabric from the dye vat and allow it to oxidise for 15 minutes. Rinse with cold water running away from the white section. Cover your rinsed peaks with plastic food wrap (this will protect them from the second dye) and secure with rubber bands. Prepare your fibre-reactive dye as per the instructions on page 18. Add the bound piece for 30 minutes. Remove, rinse, unbind and rinse again until the water runs clear.

Project: Kumo duvet cover and pillowcases

A great project to decorate your bedroom or give old bedding a new lease on life. Kumo can be used in different sizes and repeats to create a unique bedding collection.

This project involves indigo dye, but would also work with a fibre-reactive or direct dye.

1 Lay out your white or lightly coloured cotton duvet cover, right-side up. Find the centre of your duvet cover and lift up to the desired size of your kumo circle. Place a rubber band at the base to secure.

2 Wet the gathered area to just above the rubber band. Using synthetic thread, wind tightly from the base of the circle to the tip and back down again, forming a large gathered circle. Secure the thread with a knot and cut the end.

3 Soak the gathered circle in a bucket of water for 20 minutes.

4 Prepare your synthetic indigo vat by filling up a tub with 15 litres (4 gallons) of warm water. Sprinkle in your indigo powder and sodium hydrosulphite. Stir gently. Dissolve your soda ash in 30 ml (2 tablespoons) of hot water. Slowly add this solution to the dye vat. Leave for 15 minutes.

5 Remove the fabric from the water and dab the excess water with a towel. Holding the fabric securely at the base of the rubber band, submerge the entire gathered circle in the dye vat for 10 minutes (you may have to hold it or drape it over the side).

6 Remove and be careful not to mark the white areas with dye. Rinse with cold water running away from the white section until the water runs clear. Undo the binding and wash with dishwashing liquid and cold water.

Contemporary kumo

To complement your duvet cover, you can create some mis-matched kumo pillowcases. Experiment with mapping out your kumo circles, clusters of kumo circles and random scattered circles.

When using indigo for bedding, it is recommended that you soak the piece in a bucket of boiling water after dyeing. This removes any excess dye particles and prevents dye transfer.

Never wash indigo-dyed pieces with laundry detergent; always use dishwashing liquid.

Heat-setting fabric

Often the beauty of shibori is in the binding and its three-dimensional state. It is sometimes difficult to imagine undoing all your intricate bindings, since the sculptural form can be just as amazing as the finished cloth. While you can also dye heat-set fabrics, this technique emphasises the sculptural aspect of this age-old craft.

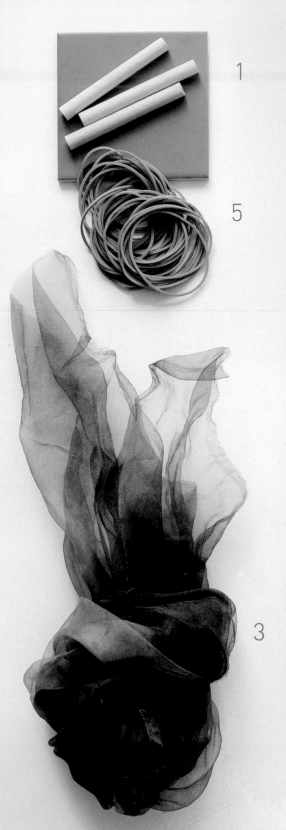

1

5

3

To heat-set fabric, 100% polyester fabric is bound, as if it is about to be put in a dye vat. Instead, the material is subjected to heat, in a receptacle such as a steamer or pressure cooker. This sets the binding in place and maintains the beautiful sculptural qualities that are lost when the focus is on the dyeing, and the binding is unwrapped and fabric ironed.

Polyester is a thermoplastic material, meaning that when heat is applied, the fibres meld and fix into place. Silk can also be used for this technique by boiling or steaming the fabric, and then allowing the piece to dry in the bound form. However, the effects are not as permanent, and items should be dry cleaned to prevent them from losing their shape.

Several artists focus on this technique, exploring the form created by shibori rather than the two-dimensional pattern created by the dye. The use of heat-set shibori is commonly found on scarves and couture blouses, where the fashion designer uses the relief qualities as a feature for his/her piece.

you will need

Tailor's chalk (1)

Ruler (2)

Piece of 100% polyester fabric (3)

Marbles (4)

Rubber bands (5)

Newspaper or muslin (6)

Old bamboo steamer (7)

Old wok

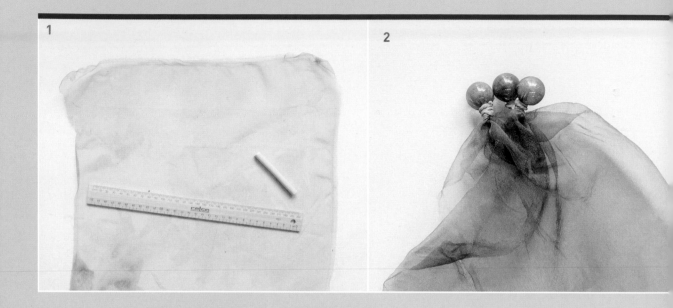

How to heat-set your fabric

1 Using tailor's chalk and a ruler, mark the area you wish to bind. (This is not essential, since you may wish to randomly scatter or cluster your design.)

2 Following the marked-out areas, place a marble on the underside of the cloth and bind with a rubber band.

3 Repeat until you have bound all your marked areas. Be sure to keep them all on the same side of the cloth, because this will affect the shape of the overall piece.

4 Wrap the bound piece in newspaper or muslin to protect it.

5 Place the piece in your bamboo steamer. Sit the steamer in the wok and fill with enough boiling water to cover the base of the steamer but not touch the piece. Steam the piece for 20 minutes. Keep an eye on the water level – you may need to add more water to prevent the wok from boiling dry.

6 Remove the steamer from the wok, allow the piece to cool and then remove it from the steamer.

7 Unwrap the piece from the newspaper and remove a marble to test the shape of the fabric. If you are happy with the heat-set piece, continue to remove the bands. If your fabric is thick or very large, it may require another 10 minutes of steaming. If this is the case, re-band the test marble and continue to steam.

8 Your piece is now finished and may be washed in cold water, if desired.

Project: High-fashion heat-set scarf

Fine, heat-set pleats create a beautiful, intricate scarf that is worthy of a feature in any fashion runway show or magazine.

When practising heat-set shibori, remember that synthetics are thermoplastic materials and get very hot.

1 Lay a sheet of plastic food wrap on a flat surface. Place your 100% synthetic organza of the same size on top.

2 Pleat the fabric horizontally with approximately 1-cm (½-inch) accordion pleats, using the plastic food wrap to hold the pleats in place.

3 Continue along the length of the fabric.

4 Carefully clamp each end of your pleated fabric and wrap, holding the pleats firmly together.

5 Place the piece in your bamboo steamer. Sit the steamer in the wok and fill with enough boiling water to cover the base of the steamer but not touch the piece. Steam the piece for 20 minutes. Keep an eye on the water level – you may need to add more water to prevent the wok from boiling dry.

6 Remove the steamer from the wok, allow the piece to cool, and then remove it from the steamer.

7 When the fabric has cooled, open the pleats and remove the plastic food wrap to reveal your heat-set pleated scarf. Your piece is now finished and may be washed in cold water, if desired.

Heat-setting and fabrics

This technique can also be done using silk or cotton fabric; however, in order to maintain your pleats, it would be a dry-clean-only item, as washing would remove the pleats, returning the fabric to its previous state.

Many fashion designers have used this technique in their collections, with Japanese fashion icon Issey Miyake being one of the first to bring it to the world's attention.

Pleating stripes

Stripes are a classic design found in many industries, and in many different styles. The notion of creating a hand-made stripe, reflecting the decisions that the creator has made, makes shibori stripes very special.

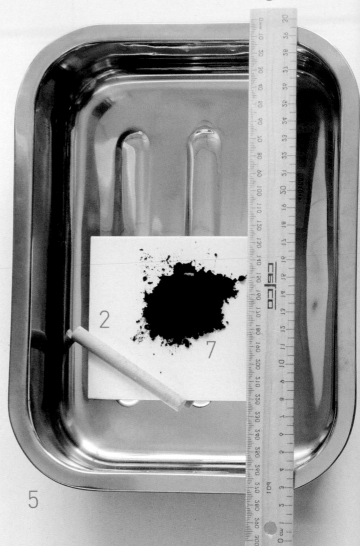

While it is possible to create stripes using other techniques such as arashi (see page 36) and shape resists (see page 76), the most basic process can be the most satisfying. This stripe technique follows a similar process to a shape resist, but without the shape. The folding techniques are used to create the stripe, and the clamps are used to hold it in place, but the effect is achieved by simply dipping half the pleated fabric into the dye.

This technique has a strong design element, because you can largely determine your final product before beginning. It is therefore important to plan your stripes. They can be altered through the size of the fold, the areas that are dipped, the angle of the pleats and whether other techniques are included, such as double stitching.

Stripes can be all different widths, two-tone or multicoloured, ombré, strong or tonal, or bleeding. There are so many variations within this simple technique. It is a great place to start, and you are sure to achieve professional results, even as a beginner. Stripes are timeless and shibori allows you to make yours personal.

you will need

Iron

Piece of white or lightly coloured cotton (1)

Tailor's chalk (2)

Ruler (3)

Pegs or clamps (4)

Soaking bucket

Towel

Shallow dye tub wide enough to accommodate the length of the stripe (5)

Paper mask

Rubber gloves (6)

Fibre-reactive dye (7)

Creating dyed stripes

1 Iron the piece of fabric, then lay it down on a hard surface.

2 Using tailor's chalk and a ruler, draw horizontal lines on your fabric 10 cm (4 inches) apart.

3 Accordion pleat the ruled lines by folding the fabric one way and then the other, ironing each pleat into place.

4 Secure the pleats together with clamps.

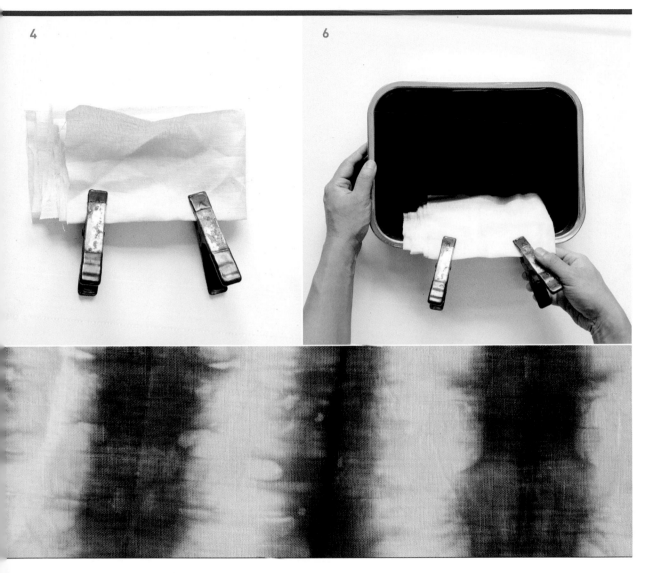

4

6

5 Soak the fabric in a bucket of water for 10 minutes. Remove from the water and dab the excess water with a towel.

6 Prepare your fibre-reactive dye by dissolving it in just enough warm water to make a solution, and add it to a shallow tub containing 1 litre (2 pints) of water. Dissolve salt and soda ash separately in hot water and add to the tub (see fibre-reactive recipe on page 18 for guidance on amounts). Holding the clamps, drape the edge of the pleats into the tub. The stripe will be double the level dipped when it is unfolded. Leave for 30 minutes.

7 Once the dye process is complete, carefully remove the fabric, making sure you do not mark the white area with the dye.

8 Rinse under cold running water, then remove the clamps. Rinse again until the water runs clear.

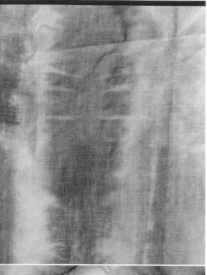

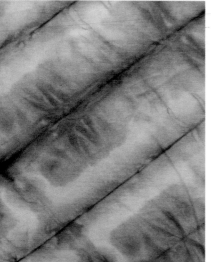

1 Two-colour dyes

Stripes in two colours look very effective.

Iron your fabric. Rule lines on your fabric with tailor's chalk at 10-cm (4-inch) intervals, accordion pleat these lines and iron into place. Secure with clamps.

Place the fabric in a soaking bucket for 10 minutes. Prepare your fibre-reactive dye as per the instructions on page 18. Remove your piece from the soaking bucket and wipe off the excess water with a towel. Holding the clamps, drape the edge of your pleats in the shallow dye tub (remember, the stripe will be double the level dipped when it is unfolded). Leave for 30 minutes.

Carefully remove the fabric, making sure you do not get the white area in the dye. Holding the clamps, rinse the dyed area under cold water. Then swap the clamps to the side that has just been dyed. Prepare the second dye colour according to the instructions and repeat the process, draping the white side of the fabric into the second dye tub and leaving for 15 minutes. Then remove, rinse under cold water, undo the clamps and rinse again until the water runs clear.

---

2 Over-dyed

This technique allows you to add to a coloured fabric you already love.

Start with a coloured fabric of a light tone. Lay your fabric flat and iron. Using a ruler and tailor's chalk, rule lines on your fabric at 10-cm (4-inch) intervals, accordion pleat these lines and iron into place. Secure with clamps.

Place the fabric in a soaking bucket for 10 minutes. Prepare your fibre-reactive dye by dissolving it in a small amount of warm water and then add to a pot containing 2 litres (4 pints) of water. Dissolve salt and soda ash in hot water and add to the pot. Pour into a dye tub. Remove your piece from the soaking bucket and wipe off the excess water with a towel. Holding the clamps, drape the edge of your pleats into the shallow dye tub (remember, the stripe will be double the level dipped when it is unfolded) and leave for 30 minutes.

Once the dye process is complete, carefully remove the fabric, making sure you do not get the white area in the dye. Rinse under cold water, undo the clamps and rinse again until the water runs clear.

---

3 Bound

This is a super-easy example of how to produce abstract stripes with lots of texture.

Lay the fabric on a flat surface. Using both hands at either end of the fabric, gather it together as if you were creating small, messy accordion pleats, then bind extremely tightly with rubber bands at 7.5-cm (3-inch) intervals.

Place the fabric in a soaking bucket for 10 minutes. Prepare your fibre-reactive dye by dissolving it in a small amount of warm water. Then add it to a pot containing 2 litres (4 pints) of water. Dissolve salt and soda ash in hot water and add to the pot.

Submerge your bound piece and leave for 30 minutes. Then remove, rinse under cold water, unbind and rinse again until the water runs clear. Notice how you have stronger lines where your resist was and softer ones where the fabric was scrunched.

Project: Striped sarong

Step away from the basic straight stripe and add a bit of fun with this quirky, hot-pink diamond version. It only takes an extra fold or two to take this sarong from a strip of cotton to a vacation in the Maldives.

The beauty of stripes is that their simplicity is timeless.

1 Fold the white or lightly coloured sarong in half horizontally and in half again vertically.

2 Beginning from the folded centre corner, iron 10-cm (4-inch) accordion pleats on a 45-degree angle until you are left with a fully pleated strip.

3 Secure one side of the strip with clamps to hold the pleats and soak the fabric in a bucket of water for 10 minutes. Remove from the water and dab the excess water with a towel.

4 Prepare your fibre-reactive dye by dissolving it in just enough warm water to make a solution. Add it to a pot filled with 2 litres (4 pints) of water. Dissolve salt and soda ash separately in hot water and add to the pot (see fibre-reactive recipe on page 18 for guidance on amounts).

5 Pour 6 cm (2½ inches) of dye solution into a shallow dye tub large enough to accommodate the length of the pleated strip.

6 Holding your clamps, carefully place one side of the pleated strip into the dye and leave for 1 hour.

7 Carefully remove from the dye, making sure you do not mark the white area with the dye, and rinse with cold water running away from the white side. Undo the clamps and rinse again until the water runs clear.

Pleats and pre-soaking

When using the pleated stripes technique, you are advised to check between the pleats while dyeing to make sure that the dye is penetrating between the folds. If an item has not been soaked correctly beforehand, areas will remain dry and this will cause uneven stripes.

Pre-soaking is a vital step in the dyeing process, as it aids in the even spread of your dye and avoids blotchy marks. Since fabric shrinks when it is wet, pre-soaking your bound pieces is recommended as it allows you to check the tension of your resist. If your bindings are loose, it is better to find out at this stage than when the dyeing process is complete.

4

Itajime
Shape resist

Itajime is a shape-resist technique. It is one of the most exciting and versatile tie-dye/shibori techniques. By folding fabric and clamping shapes into place, you can create patterns as basic or as intricate as you desire.

Shape-resist shibori uses two flat shapes sandwiched together to form a resist on the fabric. These shapes need to be held securely with either clamps, rubber bands or twine. The device you choose to hold the shapes will determine the effect you get between the shape pattern. Using clamps will leave a clean space between your shapes, but using bands or twine will form another resist leaving fine lines, giving additional texture to your piece.

The beauty of itajime is that you, the creator, are given the option to plan your design. Depending on the desired result, you can design a piece that is very structured and geometric with fine lines, or a loosely folded artistic piece with lots of soft bleeding dye textures. It is important to consider the fabric choice when using the shape-resist technique; if the fabric is too thick, the resist will not be secure enough to prevent the dye from penetrating.

Itajime shibori relies on a fold whereby the fabric is folded back and forth, resembling an accordion. This fold ensures that the fabric is always on the outside rather than being folded upon itself, making sure the dye can evenly penetrate. This fold also provides a pattern, and the size of your pleats will determine the spacing between your shape pattern.

5

you will need

Rubber gloves (1)

Paper mask

Spoon (2)

Fibre-reactive dye (3)

Dye tub

Iron

White or lightly coloured natural-fibre cloth (4)

Two matching resist shapes (5)

Clamps, rubber bands or twine (6)

Soaking bucket

Tongs for removing your fabric from dye (7)

Dishwashing liquid

Salt

Soda ash

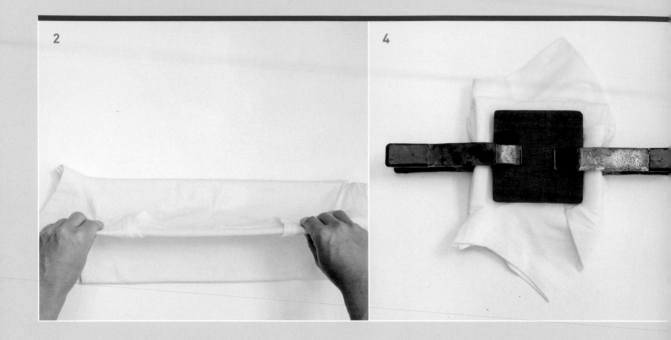

How to tie-dye using shape resists

1 Iron your fabric. In this example, we use a cotton T-shirt (see also the T-shirt project on pages 82–83).

2 Begin pleating your fabric horizontally. The size of your pleat is determined by the size of your resist shape and hence the spacing of your geometric pattern.

3 You now need to repeat this fold on the vertical to create a square shape.

4 Place your fabric between your two matching shapes, and ensure your shapes are perfectly lined up, creating a resist. Secure the shapes in place with your clamps, twine or rubber bands.

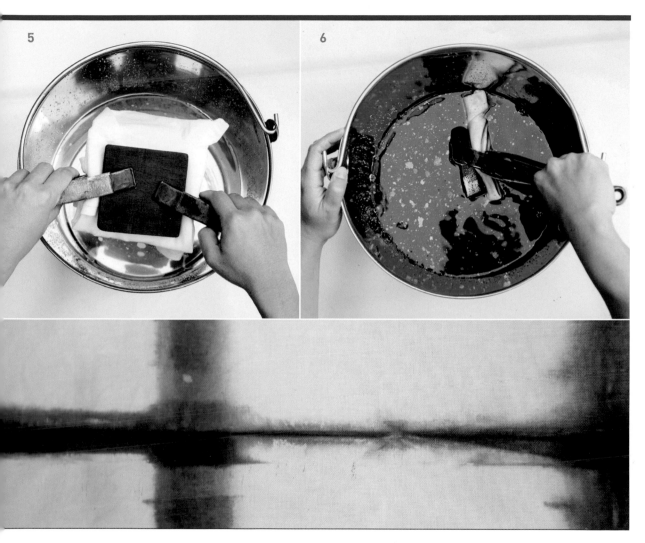

5 Leave to soak in a bucket of water for several minutes, ensuring the fabric is completely wet. This fills the fibres of your fabric, which means you will get a more even dye result and the dye is less likely to rush in and penetrate your resist.

NOTE: It is a good idea to ensure your clamps and bands are tight enough at this point, as fabric shrinks when wet.

6 Prepare your fibre-reactive dye by dissolving it in just enough warm water to make a solution, and add it to a pot containing 2 litres (4 pints) of water. Dissolve salt and soda ash separately in hot water and add to the pot (see fibre-reactive recipe on page 18 for guidance on amounts). Place your wet fabric item in your dye pot, making sure the item is fully immersed.

7 Leave for 15 minutes, stirring occasionally.

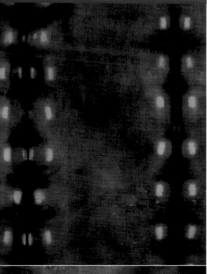

1 Pegging

This is a modern-day version of shape resist, as it is highly effective and simple to do using household clothes pegs. Here is a piece of lightweight cotton dyed using indigo dye.

Pleat your fabric horizontally with folds of approximately 10 cm (4 inches). Re-pleat vertically, with folds of approximately 10 cm (4 inches) to create a square shape. Place as many clothes pegs on the two sides of the square as you wish. We love the look of just a few; it is simple, elegant and very Japanese inspired.

Soak in warm water for 5 minutes. Prepare your synthetic indigo dye vat as per the instructions on page 18. Gently place your fabric in your indigo vat. Leave for 15 minutes without agitating. Remove and allow to oxidise for 15 minutes.

Rinse thoroughly before taking off your clothes pegs. Rinse any residual dye, remove the clothes pegs, and unfold. Wash with dishwashing liquid.

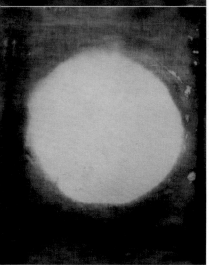

2 Circles

Circle shape resist can be done using craft shapes or simple jar lids.

The size of your pleat is determined by the size of your resist shape and hence the spacing of your geometric pattern. This example uses a 12-cm (4¾-inch) deep pleat and 10-cm (4-inch) jar lids on 50 cm (20 inches) of lightweight cotton.

Begin pleating your fabric horizontally. You now need to re-pleat this fold on the vertical to create a square shape. Place your fabric between your matching 10-cm (4-inch) jar lids, secure with clamps and soak in warm water for 5 minutes. Prepare your synthetic indigo dye vat as per the instructions on page 18. Gently place your fabric in your indigo vat. Leave for 15 minutes without agitating. Remove and allow to oxidise for 15 minutes.

Rinse thoroughly before taking off your circle resist. Rinse any residual dye, remove the lids, and unfold. Wash with dishwashing liquid.

3 Triangles

This triangular geometric pattern is really popular and fun to do. You'll need two flat triangle shapes to create the resist.

Pleat the fabric horizontally, with folds of approximately 10 cm (4 inches), then, instead of folding your fabric vertically into a square shape, you must replicate the triangle shapes being used as a resist. Fold your fabric back and forth following the line of your triangle shape, much like making samosas! See page 22 for diagrams.

Place your fabric between your matching 10-cm (4-inch) triangle shapes, secure with clamps and soak in warm water for 5 minutes. Prepare your synthetic indigo dye vat as per the instructions on page 18. Gently place your fabric in your indigo vat. Leave for 15 minutes without agitating. Remove and allow to oxidise for 15 minutes.

Rinse thoroughly before taking off your triangle resists. Rinse any residual dye, remove the shapes and unfold. Wash with dishwashing liquid.

Project: Windowpane T-shirt

This T-shirt was dyed using indigo dye, which is very good for shape resist because it is a surface dye (it sits on the surface of the fibre) and creates some great tones and textures.

The sleeves of the T-shirt are left out of the fold in order for them to remain solid blue. Since a T-shirt has a front and a back and is quite thick, large squares are used for the resist in order to keep folding to a minimum.

1 Pleat your T-shirt horizontally, with folds of approximately 14 cm (5½ inches).

2 You now need to re-pleat this fold on the vertical to create a square shape; again, the pleat fold is 14 cm (5½ inches) deep.

3 Place your T-shirt between your matching 12-cm (4¾-inch) squares and secure with clamps, leaving the sleeves out.

4 Prepare your synthetic indigo dye vat as per the instructions on page 18. Place the T-shirt in the vat and leave for 15 minutes.

5 Remove and allow to oxidise for 15 minutes.

6 Rinse thoroughly before taking off your square resists. Rinse any residual dye, remove the square resists and unfold.

7 Wash with dishwashing liquid and rinse until the water runs clear. Hang on the line to dry.

Indigo dye

Indigo dye is a natural dye used all over the world that is well known for its distinctive blue colour. It is most commonly used for the dyeing of denim jeans. Indigo dye belongs to the dye family known as vat dyes. It is not soluble in water; to be dissolved, it must undergo a chemical change. Your dyed item is always green when first removed from your indigo vat. After several minutes of being exposed to air, the dyed fabric changes from green to blue. This is known as oxidising (reacting with the oxygen in the air). While making an indigo vat is more work than many of the other commercial dyes available, it is well worth the effort because the results are unique and the process is fascinating. Items dyed with indigo should always be washed with dishwashing liquid to prevent dye transfer.

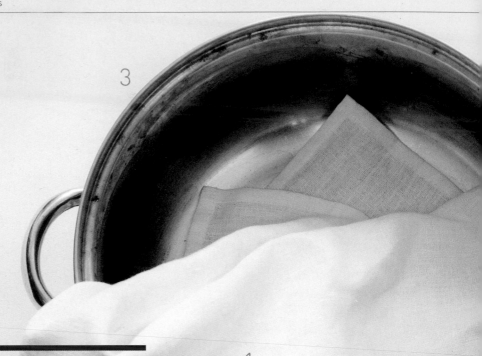

3

1

Scrunch

The simplest technique is often the most effective. With scrunch, fabric is gathered or scrunched randomly and bound with twine or rubber bands before being dyed. The pattern is random and abstract, with directional branch-like lines revealing themselves throughout the fabric.

The tension of the binding in scrunch dyeing determines the amount of pattern or texture on the piece. If it is too tight, no colour can seep in, leaving very little pattern. If it is too loose, the dye will penetrate through, leaving very little texture. The tension of the bands or twine will inform the design and leave a delicate imprint of the binding resist.

The beauty of the technique is that you can choose to plunge into the unknown, scrunching and binding at random and then unwrapping an intricate surprise at the end. At the other end of the spectrum, as you master the technique, you can direct your design and start to influence the results.

Scrunch dyeing has a strong fashion application because it can be easily used with unusually shaped garments, which may be difficult to pleat or fold. The aesthetic can be very soft and

subtle, or strong and striking. If you aren't happy with your results, you can rescrunch. Start soft and then add layers if you're not sure what you want. However, the unexpected results may provide what you never knew you were after. Always remember: it may not be until you are ironing the dry fabric that the beauty of shibori is revealed.

Scrunch can be one colour or multi-coloured. If you are using a fibre-reactive dye, you may want to utilise some of the space-dyeing techniques on pages 108–113. Pouring colour into different sections of your scrunch gives bursts of random colour, and when done subtly, it makes an interesting feature piece. Indigo is highly effective with this technique, since it gives many different levels of tone that add to the random pattern.

2

4

you will need

Cotton or natural-
fibre fabric (1)

Rubber bands or
twine (2)

Soaking bucket

Towel

Paper mask

Rubber gloves

Dye tub (3)

Fibre-reactive dye (4)

Salt

Soda ash

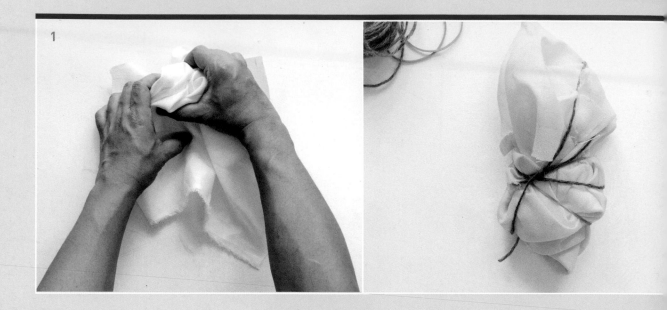

How to scrunch dye

1 Gather your fabric and bunch it together in a random fashion.

2 Secure each scrunch with rubber bands or twine.

3 Soak the fabric in a bucket of water for 15 minutes. Remove from the water and dab the excess water with a towel.

4 Check your bands or twine are tight enough to resist the dye; when the cloth is wet, it shrinks.

5 Fill the dye tub with 15 litres (4 gallons) warm water per 500g (17 oz) dry fabric. Prepare your fibre-reactive dye by dissolving it in a small amount of warm water and then add it to the tub. Dissolve salt and soda ash in hot water and add to the tub.

6 Leave for approximately 20 minutes.

7 Once the dye process is complete, remove the fabric from the dye tub, rinse under cold running water and then remove the binding. Rinse again until the water runs clear.

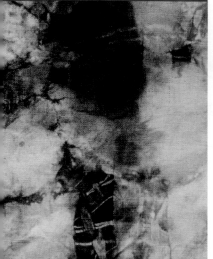

1 Twice dyed

Using two colours with this technique creates depth and a variety of hues.

Gather your fabric randomly and bunch it together. Secure it with rubber bands or twine. Place the fabric in a soaking bucket for 15 minutes. Remove your piece from the soaking bucket, wipe off the excess water with a towel and check that your bands or twine are tight enough to resist the dye, in case of fabric shrinkage.

Fill your dye tub with 2 litres (4 pints) of water per 100g (17 oz) of dry fabric. Prepare the lighter-coloured dye by dissolving it in a small amount of boiling water, then pour it into the dye tub. Dissolve salt and soda ash in hot water and add to the tub. Submerge your fabric in the dye tub for approximately 20 minutes. Rinse the bound piece under cold water with the resists still intact. Undo the fabric, rescrunch and secure again with bands or twine. Mix up the darker-coloured dye as you did the lighter one and add it to a second dye tub. Dissolve soda ash and salt and add to the tub. Add the bound piece and leave for 15 minutes.

Then remove, unbind and rinse under cold water until the water runs clear.

2 Scrunch with indigo dye

The scrunch technique allows indigo to truly express itself in its form as a stunning surface pattern.

Gather your fabric randomly and bunch it together. Secure with bands or twine. Place the fabric in a soaking bucket for 15 minutes. Remove your piece from the soaking bucket, wipe off the excess water with a towel and check that your bands or twine are tight enough to resist the dye, in case of fabric shrinkage. If you can get your fingers under the twine or bands, they are not tight enough to resist the dye.

Prepare the synthetic indigo vat according to the instructions on page 18. Submerge your fabric in the dye tub for approximately 15 minutes. Remove the fabric and allow to oxidise for 15 minutes.

Rinse the bound piece under cold water until the water runs clear, then unbind and rinse again.

3 Placement scrunch

Using the scrunch technique in just a selected area can add dramatic effect to a garment.

Select an area on your cloth or pre-made clothing item. Gather your fabric randomly and bunch it together. Secure with bands or twine. Place the fabric in a soaking bucket for 15 minutes. If you wish to keep the unbound area white, or the original fabric colour, it is a good idea to protect it with a plastic bag that can hang outside the dye tub.

Fill your dye tub with 2 litres (4 pints) of water per 100g (17 oz) of dry fabric. Prepare the dye by dissolving it in a small amount of boiling water, then pour it into the dye tub. Dissolve salt and soda ash in hot water and add to the pot. Remove your piece from the soaking bucket and wipe off the excess water with a towel. Submerge your fabric in the dye tub for approximately 30 minutes.

Remove and rinse the bound piece under cold water until the water runs clear, then unbind and rinse again.

Project: Boutique indigo tablecloth

Stunning textures and beautiful tones and lines can be achieved on large-scale pieces to make a tablecloth perfect for entertaining. Two levels of scrunch give depth by adding layers of tone to the piece using different shades of the same dye.

It is important to always check the tightness of your rubber bands or twine; if it is too loose, too much dye will penetrate through and your scrunch will lack definition.

1   Gather and scrunch areas of your tablecloth and secure tightly with rubber bands or twine. Leave enough room to include further scrunches of a second level or shade.

2   Soak your bound tablecloth in a soaking bucket for 40 minutes.

3   Prepare your synthetic indigo dye vat according to the instructions on page 18.

4   Remove your bound tablecloth from the soaking bucket, wipe off excess water with a towel and carefully lower it into your indigo vat. Leave for 15 minutes, without agitating.

5   Carefully remove the tablecloth from the indigo vat and allow to oxidise in a bucket for 15 minutes. Your tablecloth will now turn from green to blue.

6   Rinse the tablecloth under water without removing the bindings. Re-scrunch the extra cloth around your bound areas. Add more bands to tightly secure. Your tablecloth should now be very small and tightly bound.

7   Place back in the indigo dye vat. Leave for 15 minutes. Remove and leave to oxidise in a bucket for 15 minutes.

8   Rinse the bound piece under cold water until the water runs clear. Unbind, rinse again and wash with dishwashing liquid.

Scrunch tips

The scrunch technique is a great technique to use for larger, bulkier items, as it does not require intricate pleats or stitches.

Indigo is a surface dye and works with layers of colour. It is said that the optimum darkness is achieved after 20 minutes in the dye tub; however, removing the piece and allowing it to oxidise before returning it to the tub again builds layers of colour, adding darker shades.

While this two-tone scrunch technique works well with all colours, it looks particularly striking with a neutral colour scheme such as black and grey.

Yanagi
Willow tree patterns

'Yanagi' is Japanese for willow. The delicate lines resemble the lines of the willow trees often seen in Japan. Yanagi is a technique that uses two distinct resists simultaneously – pleating and rope – to produce a collaboration of pattern.

In the yanagi technique, the cloth is pleated in knife pleats before being bound around a thick rope and secured with twine. The overwhelming appearance can be a tonal patchwork of boxes where the lines of twine and rope meet, but on closer inspection, these resists are soft with subtle discrepancies, movement and the exposure of bind lines.

The knife pleat is the most common sewing pleat. It is a single pleat turned in one direction, like steps. This pleat is used in yanagi because it protects one layer, which is underneath, and exposes another layer. The fabric is then bound around a rope because it provides a flexible base that can be manipulated in order to fit into a dye tub. The rope can also be rolled around itself in a snail-like manner, adding another level of texture. Twine is used to secure the cloth along the rope at regular intervals or with random spacing, depending on your individual style. The thickness of your twine will also impact your finished result, leaving heavy and thick resist lines or fine and delicate lines in its path.

This is a more advanced technique for people who are patient and precise, and want to see the labours of their work in the detail of their fabric. The freedom is left to the artist to decide the best materials, pleat sizes and pleat styles, as well as twine size, binding technique, dye colours and colour placement. By changing these variables, yanagi can continue to surprise the creator.

3

4

you will need

Iron

Cotton or natural-fibre fabric, approximately 30 x 50 cm (12 x 20 inches) (1)

NOTE: The size of your fabric is determined by the size of your rope. Ideally, your pleated fabric will fit around the rope without overlapping to avoid ghosting or masked-out patterns.

55 cm (22 inches) of thick rope, approximately 4.5 cm (1¾ inches) diameter (2)

Rubber bands

Synthetic thread (3)

Soaking bucket

Paper mask

Rubber gloves (4)

Towel

Dye tub

Fibre-reactive dye (5)

Salt

Soda ash

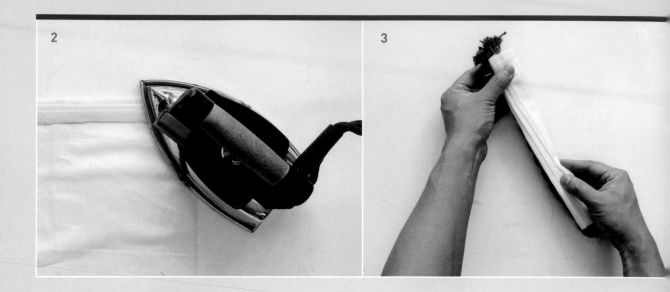

How to achieve yanagi patterning

1 Iron the piece of fabric, then lay it down on a hard surface.

2 Iron 1-cm (½-inch) pleats into your fabric. It is very important that your pleats are all in one direction. You may choose to mark out your pleat intervals with tailor's chalk; however, the organic nature of this design lends itself to uneven pleats.

3 Lay your fabric along the length of the rope.

4 Secure the ends of the pleated fabric to either end of the rope with rubber bands.

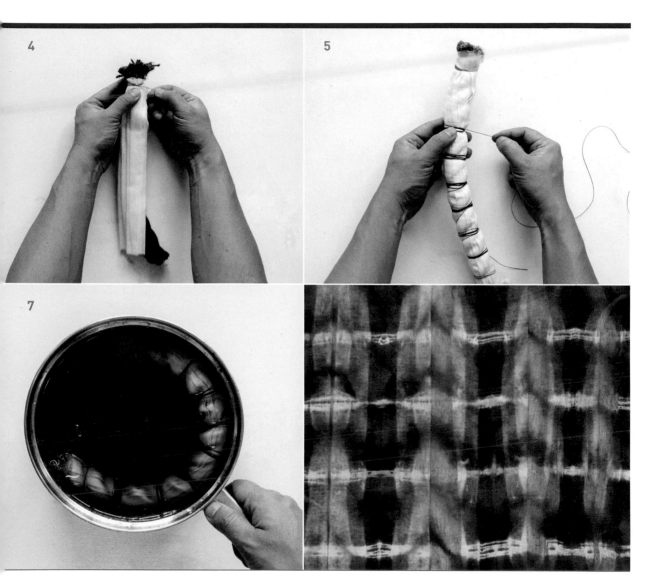

5 Tie the synthetic thread securely to one end of the rope. Wind the thread firmly around the fabric-covered rope at random intervals. Continue down the length of the rope, tying it securely at the bottom.

6 Soak the fabric in a bucket of water for 15 minutes. Remove from the water and dab the excess water with a towel.

7 Prepare your fibre-reactive dye by dissolving it in just enough warm water to create a solution, and add it to a pot containing 2 litres (4 pints) of water. Dissolve salt and soda ash separately in hot water and add to the pot (see fibre-reactive recipe on page 18 for guidance on amounts). Leave for a maximum of 30 minutes, agitating regularly.

8 Once the dye process is complete, remove the fabric from the dye pot, rinse under cold running water and then remove the binding. Rinse again until the water runs clear.

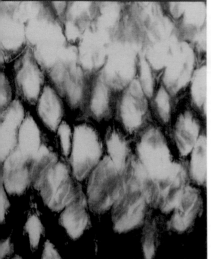

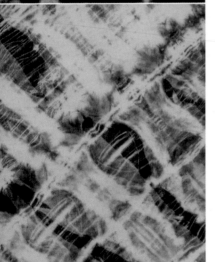

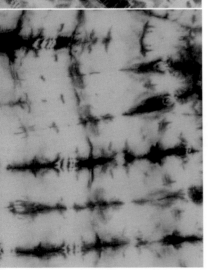

1 Honeycomb

This pattern is beautiful, unexpected, simple, effective and as delicious as a honeycomb itself.

Lay your fabric on a flat surface. Place a piece of string horizontally across the bottom and ensure that it extends 2.5 cm (1 inch) longer than the fabric on each side. Loosely roll your fabric over the string so that your fabric forms a loose sleeve with the string in the middle. Tie the two ends of the string together in a tight knot. This method will cause the material to gather and scrunch.

Place your scrunchie-like piece in a soaking bucket for 20 minutes. Prepare the synthetic indigo vat according to the instructions on page 18. Remove your piece from the soaking bucket and wipe off the excess water with a towel. Submerge your fabric in the dye vat for approximately 15 minutes.

Remove the fabric and allow it to oxidise for 15 minutes. Rinse the bound piece under cold water until the water runs clear, before unbinding and rinsing again.

2 Diagonal

Play with the elements of design; this is classic yanagi in a different direction.

Lay your fabric on a flat surface and iron out any creases. Iron 1-cm (½-inch) knife pleats into your fabric. Wrap your pleated fabric along the length of the rope and secure each end to the rope with rubber bands, as per the standard yanagi method (see pages 94–95). Tie synthetic twine to one end of your rope and secure with a knot. Wind the twine firmly around the fabric-covered rope at random intervals. Continue down the length of the rope, tying securely at the bottom.

Place the fabric in a soaking bucket for 15 minutes. Prepare the synthetic indigo vat according to the instructions on page 18. Remove your piece from the soaking bucket and wipe off the excess water. Submerge your fabric in the dye vat for approximately 10 minutes.

Remove the fabric and allow it to oxidise for 15 minutes. Rinse the bound piece under cold water until the water runs clear, before unbinding and rinsing again.

3 Compressed

Through this mixture of techniques, arashi and yanagi, a new pattern is achieved with finer details and tonal variations.

Lay your fabric out flat and iron. Iron 1-cm (½-inch) knife pleats into your fabric. Wrap the pleated fabric along the length of the rope and secure each end to the rope with rubber bands, as per the standard yanagi method (see pages 94–95). Add rubber bands down the length of the rope at random intervals, compressing the fabric towards one end of the rope as you go, and securing.

Place the fabric in a soaking bucket for 15 minutes. Prepare the synthetic indigo vat according to the instructions on page 18. Remove your piece from the soaking bucket and wipe off the excess water. Submerge your fabric in the dye vat for approximately 15 minutes.

Remove the fabric and allow it to oxidise for 15 minutes. Rinse the bound piece under cold water until the water runs clear, before unbinding and rinsing again.

Project: Yanagi apron

Decorating your old stained apron is easy, and a busy pattern like yanagi will make it an item you'll want to wear to inspire you on all your creative projects.

The traditional pattern of yanagi is delicate and fine, but by adapting the size of pleats or folds, you can modify this technique to accommodate the shape of a pre-made item.

1 Lay your apron on a flat surface and iron out any creases.

2 Iron 2.5-cm (1-inch) knife pleats into your apron.

3 Wrap your pleated fabric along the length of the rope and secure each end to the rope with rubber bands.

4 Tie synthetic twine to one end of the rope and secure with a knot. Wind the twine firmly around the fabric-covered rope at random intervals.

5 Continue down the length of the rope, tying securely at the bottom.

6 Place the apron in a soaking bucket for 30 minutes.

7 Prepare your synthetic indigo dye vat according to the instructions on page 18.

8 Remove your apron from the soaking bucket and wipe off the excess water with a towel. Submerge your bound apron in the dye vat for approximately 15 minutes.

9 Remove carefully and allow to oxidise for 15 minutes.

10 Rinse the bound piece under cold water until the water runs clear. Unbind, rinse again and wash with dishwashing liquid.

Traditional yanagi

In traditional Japanese yanagi, the fabric is hand gathered in tiny little pleats before being bound around the rope. It is these random hand gatherings that create the unique willow-like lines. However, in this version, an iron is used to hold the pleats in place to make the technique easier for beginners.

Discharge bleaching

Discharge is removing colour, rather than adding colour. It is the reverse technique to most dyeing processes. This is exciting, because you're turning shibori upside down!

Any binding technique can be used with this process. The fabric is bound as usual, and then it is submerged in a vat of bleach rather than dye. The results will be the mirror image of what you would see if a dye vat had been used. The binding will protect the colour, and the exposed fabric will be bleached.

Cellulose fibre is the most commonly used fabric for discharge bleaching, but any natural fibre that has been pre-dyed will work well. Domestic chloride bleach and commercial discharge pastes can be used. Bleach degenerates fabric, so the process must be slowed down to minimise the risk of fabric deterioration. Discharge pastes are more difficult to source and require a much more advanced process of colouring, but they are considerably more versatile because of their paste consistency and are less tough on the fabric. The concentration of bleach or discharge paste used will also influence the bleached colour and consistency, as well as likely damage to the fabric.

This technique is used in fashion because of the popularity of the stressed appearance, particularly in denim jeans. Denim is an ideal material because it is a strong worker's fabric that is complemented by this technique.

Knowing discharge bleaching processes gives artists more creative power, since they are not limited to the dye colours they may have access to. A beautiful colour on a fabric can be maintained and a pattern can be impressed upon it using bleach.

Due to the harsh nature of the chemicals involved in bleaching, it is advisable to undertake this process outside.

you will need

Iron

Piece of pre-dyed natural-fibre cloth (1)

Two matching resist shapes (2)

Clamps (3)

Soaking bucket

Paper mask/ respirator

Rubber gloves

Bleaching bucket

Household bleach (4)

Bleach neutralising solution (see page 18)

Discharging colour

1 Iron the piece of fabric, then lay it down on a hard surface.

2 Accordion pleat the fabric horizontally into pleats of 10 cm (4 inches) by folding the fabric one way and then the other. If your aesthetic lends itself to precision, you may choose to mark out your pleat intervals with tailor's chalk.

3 Repeat the pleat vertically to create a square shape.

4 Place the fabric between the two matching resist shapes, lining them up perfectly on either side. Secure with clamps.

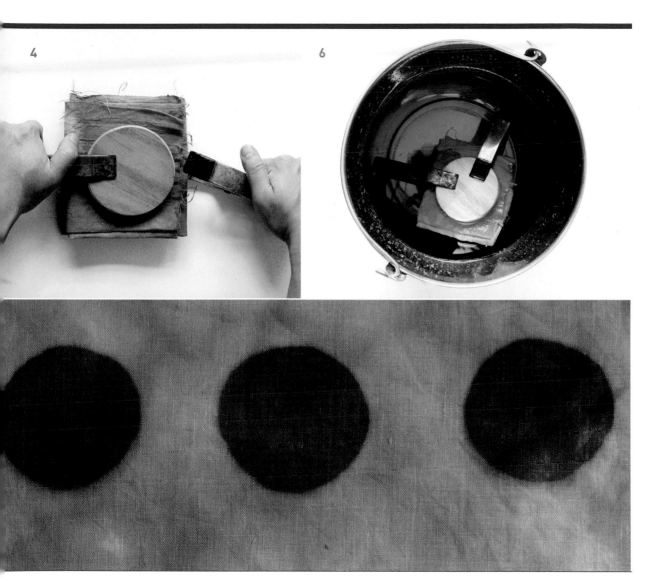

5 Place the clamped fabric in a bucket of water to soak for 20 minutes.

6 Fill a bucket with water and add 250 ml (8¾ fl oz) of household bleach. Submerge your pre-soaked piece in the bleach mix.

7 Leave the piece to discharge for approximately 2 hours, regularly agitating until the desired tone is reached.

8 Remove the piece from the bleach, remove the clamps and wash thoroughly with water. Mix up your bleach neutralising solution (1 tablespoon of sodium metabisulphite to 10 litres [2½ gallons] of water). Soak your piece for 2 hours, remove and re-rinse.

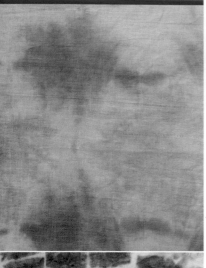

1 Soda ash

Soda ash, otherwise known as washing soda, is an alternative to using bleach. It is less harmful to your fabric, safer to use and appropriate for application on hand-dyed fabrics.

Fold your pre-dyed fabric horizontally into 10-cm (4-inch) accordion pleats. Repeat the pleat vertically, making a square shape. Secure with rubber bands horizontally and vertically (this will create a cross).

Place the fabric in a soaking bucket for 20 minutes. Fill an old, large cooking pot with enough water to accommodate the fabric and allow it to move freely. Set on the stove to boil. Add the soda ash once the water is boiling (2 tablespoons of soda ash to 1 litre [2 pints] of water). Remove your fabric from the soaking bucket and submerge it in the pot on the stove. Continue boiling for approximately 1½ hours. Check the fabric regularly until the colour is removed.

Once this has happened, remove the fabric with tongs, unbind and scrub with dishwashing liquid and water (once cool enough to handle).

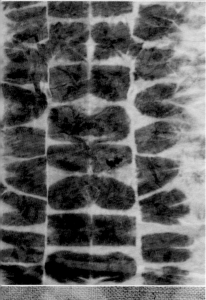

2 Boxes

This is the reverse of the boxes stitch resist method (see page 48). It is best to use a sturdy fabric such as a cotton drill, which will withstand the bleaching.

Lay your fabric out and iron. Starting from the end, fold the fabric forwards 5 cm (2 inches) and then fold this forwards twice more (maintaining the same width), in order to create four levels of fabric that are 5 cm (2 inches), with the excess fabric coming out of the side. Iron flat. Turn your piece to the side and accordion pleat the length of the folded fabric. Using a double-threaded needle, pass the needle through your accordion pleats to hold the gather. Knot the thread to secure.

Place the fabric in a soaking bucket for 20 minutes. Mix up your bleach solution (100 ml [3½ fl oz] of bleach to 250 ml [8¾ fl oz] of water). Remove the fabric from the bucket and wring out the excess water. Place it in the bucket with the bleach solution and set aside to discharge for 2 hours.

Remove the fabric with tongs, rinse thoroughly and remove the stitches. Mix up your bleach-neutralising solution (1 tablespoon of sodium metabisulphite to 10 litres [2½ gallons] of water). Soak your piece for 2 hours, remove and rinse again.

3 Bleach and over-dye using Itajime triangles

This pattern acts like an echo of a former shape.

You'll need two matching flat triangle shapes for the resist. Natural-coloured hessian has been used here. Fold the fabric horizontally with pleats of 10 cm (4 inches), and then fold your fabric back and forth following the line of your triangle shape.

Place your fabric between your 10-cm (4-inch) triangle resist shapes, secure with clamps, soak in warm water for 5 minutes and then gently place in a bucket containing your bleach solution (100 ml [3½ fl oz] of bleach to 250 ml [8¾ fl oz] of water). Leave for 2 hours or until the colour has been removed. Remove the fabric with tongs and rinse the bleach off with water. Mix up your bleach neutralising solution (1 tablespoon of sodium metabisulphite to 10 litres [2½ gallons] of water). Undo the resists and triangle folds until the fabric is in its original pleats. Re-fold the triangles in a different way and place between the resists and clamps. Prepare the fibre-reactive dye by dissolving it in warm water, then add to a large dye pot filled with warm water. Add salt and soda ash. Submerge your fabric for approximately 30 minutes. Then remove, rinse under cold water, undo the clamps and rinse again until the water runs clear.

Project: Pink dip-bleached hessian cushion cover

Mixing fabrics and textures such as hessian and playing with distressing fabric adds rustic charm.

Creating stripes with the natural colour of hessian and an extra dye colour can result in a versatile outdoor cushion.

1 Soak your pre-made hessian cushion cover in a bucket of water for 30 minutes.

2 Fill a bucket with water and add 250 ml (8¾ fl oz) of household bleach. Stir thoroughly.

3 Drape two-thirds of the cushion cover in the bleach solution, leaving the other end hanging over the side.

4 Leave the piece to discharge for 2 hours, agitating regularly.

5 Remove carefully from the bucket and wash thoroughly with water and dishwashing liquid, making sure no bleach is left on the hessian.

6 Prepare a tub of pink fibre-reactive dye as per the instructions on page 18. Drape the top third of your bleached section of the cushion cover in the bucket. Leave for 30 minutes.

7 Remove the cushion cover carefully from the bucket and rinse thoroughly with water. Mix up your bleach neutralising solution of 1 tablespoon of sodium metabisulphite to 10 litres (2½ gallons) of water and soak your bleached hessian for 2 hours. Remove from the soaking bucket and rinse again.

Discharge tips

When using bleach to remove colour, it is important to consider the fabric you are using. A strong, durable fabric like hessian or denim tolerates the bleach and gives amazing patterns and textures that are worthy of further experimentation.

If you wish to discharge a silk or more delicate cloth, consider using a discharge paste, which is a chemical activated by the use of steam. Discharge paste can be used for screen printing or fabric painting, or watered down and used with shibori to perform reverse effects on your pieces. Instead of adding colour to the unbound area you are focusing on, you keep the existing fabric colour and remove the surrounding colour.

3

4

Space dyeing

For many centuries, artists have spread bound cloth across a surface and poured dye concentrate onto certain areas to control the colour application. Space dyeing refers to this process and is the contemporary version of this old technique that does not necessarily use bound cloth, but does use drizzling, squirting and splashing! Fun and easy, this technique is perfect for everyone, including kids.

Space dyeing can be as simple as spreading a piece of fabric across a surface and pulling areas of it into small peaks. When the dye is poured over the fabric, the peaks will not be covered, and this creates differences in tone. This technique allows the artist to use multiple colours and plays on the integration and intermixing of these colours.

Space dyeing is like scrunch dyeing (see pages 84–89), but without the definitive lines that come from binding. The pattern is bolder and braver and makes for fantastic statement pieces. This is modern shibori at its best, informed by age-old techniques, but producing something unique, simple and appealing in contemporary design.

This technique begins with white or lightly coloured cloth, which is spread out in a shallow dye tub. Arranging damp, pre-treated fabric in raised peaks and swirls gives a ground on which the dye will be poured. Once the artist has mixed and prepared dye concentrates in the chosen colour palette, it is then time to drizzle, pour or squirt the dye in selected areas. The colours will intermingle and combine in an organic manner, and the raised peaks will remain clean or have bleeding dye tones.

Colour choice is the most important design element that the artist needs to consider in space dyeing, as inappropriate colour combinations can yield unwanted results. Space dyeing is the easiest of all techniques and is a great way to involve kids in the fun of tie-dye.

2

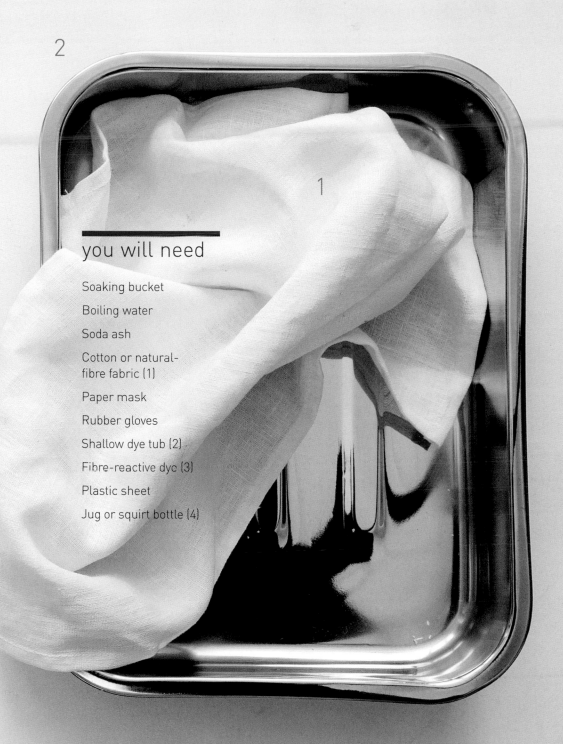

1

you will need

Soaking bucket

Boiling water

Soda ash

Cotton or natural-
fibre fabric (1)

Paper mask

Rubber gloves

Shallow dye tub (2)

Fibre-reactive dye (3)

Plastic sheet

Jug or squirt bottle (4)

How to space dye your fabric

1 Fill a bucket with boiling water and add 2 tablespoons of soda ash. Stir to dissolve.

2 Carefully put the fabric in the bucket and leave to soak for 20 minutes, stirring occasionally.

3 Remove the fabric from the bucket and wring out the excess water. Do not rinse.

4 Lay the fabric in a shallow dye tub.

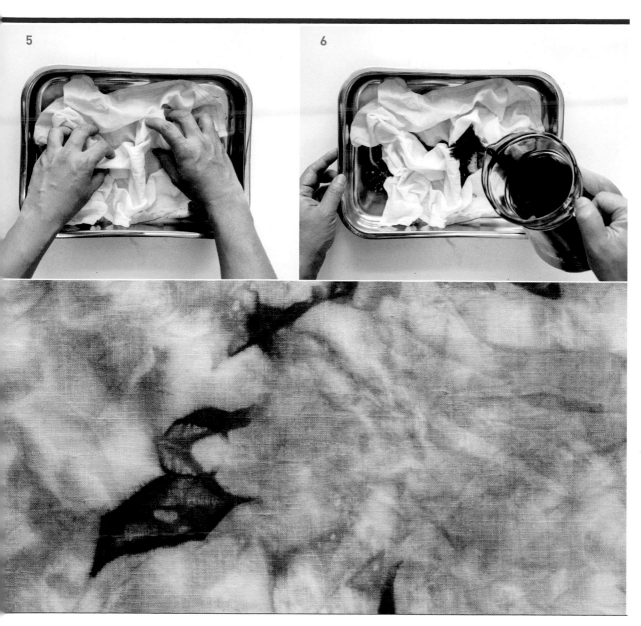

5 Arrange the fabric in raised peaks and swirls, providing areas for the dye to sit.

6 Mix up 5g (⅖ oz) of the fibre-reactive dye with 300 ml (½ pint) of warm water. Using either a squirt bottle or jug, pour the dye into the fabric folds and creases.

7 Loosely cover with the plastic sheet and leave overnight.

8 Remove the fabric from the dye tub and rinse under cold running water until the water runs clear.

1 Ice dyeing

An innovative and playful method that achieves random patterns and textures.

Freeze a number of trays of ice cubes (enough to cover the surface area of your fabric). Dissolve 2 tablespoons of soda ash in a bucket of boiling water and soak your fabric in this for 30 minutes. Remove the fabric and wring out the excess water. Arrange the fabric with peaks and folds on an old baking rack above a shallow tray to collect the melted ice.

Take the ice cubes from the freezer and place them in the desired pattern on your fabric. Choose several complementary dye colours in powder form. Using an old spoon, sprinkle the dye powder onto the ice so that all the ice is covered. Set aside in a safe place and leave the ice to melt and the magic to happen for 24 hours.

The dye is now set, and you may rinse your fabric thoroughly in cold water until it runs clear.

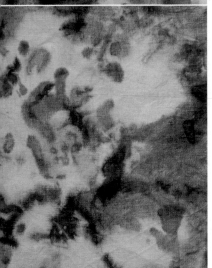

2 Two-colour dyes

A super-fun process that allows for bold colour statements – great for kids!

Soak your fabric in a bucket of boiling water and soda ash for 30 minutes. Remove from the soaking bucket and wring out the excess water. Lay your fabric in a shallow dye tub. Arrange the cloth in raised peaks and swirls, providing areas for the dye solutions to sit in. Mix up 5g (⅖ oz) of each of the fiber-reactive dyes with 300 ml (½ pint) of warm water and pour each color into one of the two separate squirt bottles or pitchers. Using the squirt bottles or jugs, apply the solutions to different areas of the fabric as you desire. Cover with plastic food wrap and leave overnight.

Remove and rinse under cold water until the water runs clear.

3 Denim

Space dyeing textures is a fun and modern way to decorate your denim with dramatic and unique results.

Lay your fabric in a shallow tub. Arrange the fabric in raised peaks and swirls, providing areas for the bleach solution to sit in. Mix up your bleach solution using 100 ml (3½ fl oz) of bleach to 250 ml (8¾ fl oz) of water. Using a squirt bottle or pitcher, apply the bleach solution to your fabric folds and creases. Set aside somewhere safe and leave to discharge for 2 hours. If you are not satisfied with the result after this time, mix a slightly stronger solution (e.g., 200 ml [7 fl oz] of bleach to 250 ml [8¾ fl oz] of water). Return the fabric to the tub until it reaches a colour you are happy with.

Once complete, rinse off the bleach thoroughly. Mix up your bleach neutralising solution (1 tablespoon of sodium metabisulphite to 10 litres [2½ gallons] of water). Soak your piece for 2 hours, remove and rinse again.

1

2

3

Project: Space-dyed table runner and napkins

The simple technique of space dyeing lends itself beautifully to creating a soft, watercolour-like pattern that adds a funky touch to any table setting. This project used pink, grey and blue fibre-reactive dyes.

When using multiple colours with space dyeing, it is important to choose colours that will work well when placed together.

1 Pre-wash your table runner and napkins before dyeing.

2 Fill a bucket with boiling water and add 2 tablespoons of soda ash. Stir to dissolve. Carefully put the runner and napkins in the bucket and leave to soak for 20 minutes, stirring occasionally.

3 Remove your items from the bucket and wring out the excess water. Do not rinse.

4 Lay your items in a shallow dye tub. Arrange the fabric in raised peaks and swirls, providing areas for the dye to sit.

5 Mix up 5g (⅖ oz) of each of the fibre-reactive dyes with 300 ml (½ pint) of warm water and pour each colour into one of the four separate squirt bottles. For this design we are using four colours of fibre-reactive dye: peach pink, indigo blue, turquoise blue and dusky grey. Using one squirt bottle at a time, pour the dye concentrate into the fabric folds and creases. Pour slowly.

6 Loosely cover with a plastic sheet and leave overnight.

7 Remove the fabric from the dye tub and rinse under cold running water until the water runs clear.

Space-dyeing tips

Fibre-reactive dyes are the most permanent of all the dyes available. This is because of the chemical reaction that takes place when soda ash is added. This creates a chemical bond with the dye, becoming a part of the fibre molecule. Pre-soaking an item in soda ash before dyeing treats the fabric, creating a base for this reaction to take place.

Fibre-reactive dyes are recommended for space dyeing your table runner and napkins, as there is a huge range of vibrant colours available and they will be sure to last a long time, despite the high level of washing.

Rust patterns

Transferring rust onto fabric to create beautiful colours and patterns is not just one of the most aesthetically pleasing techniques; it is also the most fun. Find old, rusty metals lying around in your shed and experiment!

This technique is about using rusty items as both your dye and your shape resist. There are so many different ways to use rust in dyeing. You can make clear shapes or perfect replicas on fabric that mimic the rusty item of choice, or create abstract imprints by wrapping wet fabric around items and binding in different areas. Alternative processes include submerging the bound fabric in water or resting rusty items on top of a flat, wet fabric and leaving it to dry.

This technique is less about following instructions and more about experimenting to see what you can produce. One of the most exciting things about this process is that you can make your own dye from rust. By placing old, rusty objects into water and leaving them to sit, this becomes a workable dye. Fabric can be bound using any technique in this book and then dyed with your rust concoction.

Once you are happy with the patterns on your fabric, it is important to cease the rusting process by soaking the fabric in salted water to avoid disintegration. The colours that can be achieved with rust are earthy and organic, and in tones that can rarely be replicated with synthetic dyes. This is an introduction to the world of using found objects to create your own natural dyes.

4

1

you will need

2 pieces of white or lightly coloured linen or natural-fibre cloth (1)

White wine vinegar (2)

Soaking bucket

2 plastic dust sheets

Towel

Old rusted items (3)

Weights or heavy items to weigh down your items (4)

Spray bottle

Salt (5)

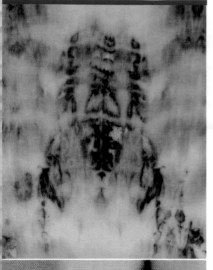

1 Wraparound rust

This technique creates an amazing abstract feature piece that texturally alludes to the shape used. Horseshoes, keys and rusty kitchen utensils are great items to use.

Soak the fabric in a bucket containing one part white wine vinegar and one part water. Use enough liquid to cover the cloth fully. Leave for approximately 1 hour. Remove the fabric from the bucket and wring out. Wrap your fabric very tightly around your chosen rusted item and secure with rubber bands. Place on a plastic dust sheet and set aside for 24 hours if a lighter shade is desired, or 3 to 5 days for a darker shade. Spray the fabric with white wine vinegar if it dries during this time. When you are happy with your rusted shade, unwrap the fabric and remove the rusted item.

Prepare a salt-water solution to neutralise the rusting process by dissolving 3 tablespoons of salt per litre (2 pints) of water and soak the fabric for 2 hours. Rinse under cold running water.

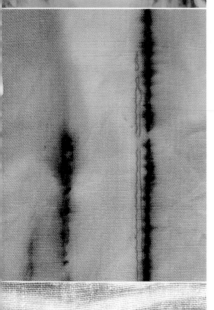

2 Rusted stripes

You can create striped rust resists using rusted poles or metal dowels.

Soak two pieces of fabric in a bucket containing one part white wine vinegar and one part water. Use enough liquid to cover the cloth fully. Leave for about 1 hour. Lay down a plastic dust sheet on a flat surface in an area that can stay undisturbed for a week (this is the dyeing time).

Remove the fabric from the bucket and wring it out. Place one piece of the fabric flat on the plastic dust sheet. Arrange the rusted items on the fabric in your chosen design. Lay the second piece of fabric over the top of the rusted items and cover with a second plastic dust sheet. Place weights on top of the plastic.

Leave to rest for a week. Check the piece twice a day. Spray the fabric with white wine vinegar if it is dry, and replace the cover and weights. When you are happy with your rusted impression, remove the rusted items. Prepare a salt-water solution to neutralise the rusting process by dissolving 3 tablespoons of salt per litre (2 pints) of water and soak the fabric for 2 hours. Rinse under cold running water.

3 Using rust with arashi

This is a contemporary take on arashi binding.

Soak the fabric in a bucket containing one part white wine vinegar and one part water. Use enough liquid to cover the cloth fully. Leave for approximately 1 hour. Remove the fabric from the bucket and wring it out. Lay your fabric on a flat surface and place a rusted pole on one end. Roll your fabric straight around the pole and secure both ends with rubber bands. Place rubber bands down the length of the pole, compressing the fabric as you go.

Protect with plastic wrap and set aside for 24 hours if a lighter shade is desired, or 3 to 5 days for a darker shade. Spray the fabric with white wine vinegar if it dries during this time. When you are happy with your rusted shade, unwrap the fabric and remove the pole.

Prepare a salt-water solution to neutralise the rusting process by dissolving 3 tablespoons of salt per litre (2 pints) of water and soak the fabric for 2 hours. Rinse under cold running water.

Project: Lucky rust horseshoe wall hanging

Rusty horseshoes make great patterns on natural linen, and experimenting with rust is a great introduction to natural dye and all its capabilities. No matter what rusted items you find around the house, it's easy to create a designer artwork that will be one of a kind and leave a lasting rusted impression.

By creating a strong geometric pattern with the rusted horseshoes you produce a stronger statement piece.

1 Soak the fabric in a bucket of half white wine vinegar and half water. Use enough liquid to cover the cloth fully. Leave for approximately 1 hour.

2 Lay a plastic dust sheet on a flat surface in an area that can stay undisturbed for a week. (This is the dyeing time.)

3 Remove the linen from the bucket, wring it out and remove the excess liquid with a towel. Place the wet linen flat on the dust sheet.

4 Arrange the rusty horseshoes in a line on half the fabric. Fold the remaining fabric over the top of the horseshoes and cover with a second plastic dust sheet. Place weights on top of the plastic to ensure optimum rust transfer and leave to rest for a week.

5 Check your piece regularly by carefully removing weights and lifting the plastic. It could take a day or two before the rust transfers to the cloth. Spray your fabric with vinegar if it is dry, and replace the cover and weights. When you are happy with your rusted texture, move the rusted horseshoes to a new line and replace the plastic dust sheet and weights. Again, check your piece regularly and maintain the moisture. You can relay your rusty items until you feel the design is complete.

6 When you are happy with your rusty design, remove the rusted items and soak the linen in a soaking bucket filled with water and 3 tablespoons of salt. Leave for 2 hours to neutralise the rusting process, rinse with cool water and hang out to dry.

Rust tips

Rust is a naturally occurring phenomenon that occurs when iron reacts with oxygen, producing a beautiful burnt orange colour. There are several ways to take advantage of this natural phenomenon, and rust transfer is one magical way.

It is also possible to dye over the top of the rust-dyed fabric. The natural orange colour looks amazing when paired with indigo, or try over-dyeing with fibre-reactive cold-water dyes to add other complementary colours.

NOTE: Rust can weaken the fibres of your fabric, so it is recommended to use the rust-dyed cloth in projects that won't be washed often.

Index